Richard H. Jahns

RAILROADS THROUGH THE COEUR D'ALENES

Railroads Through the Coeur d'Alenes

By

John V. Wood

The CAXTON PRINTERS, Ltd.
Caldwell, Idaho
1983

© 1983 by
The CAXTON PRINTERS, Ltd.
Caldwell, Idaho

Library of Congress Cataloging in Publication Data

Wood, John, 1945-
   Railroads through the Coeur d'Alenes.

   Bibliography: p.
   Includes index.
   1. Railroads — Idaho — Coeur d'Alene region.
I. Title.
TF25.C598.W66   385′.09796′94   82-4168
ISBN 0-87004-297-1   AACR2
ISBN 0-87004-291-2 (pbk.)

Lithographed and bound in the United States of America by
The CAXTON PRINTERS, Ltd.
Caldwell, Idaho 83605
137834

Dedication

I dedicate this book to the Lord Jesus who not only gave me life and this opportunity to work on something I find truly exciting, but also has taught me greater patience and faith through the experience. For the Bible proclaims in Colossians 3:17 —

> And whatsoever ye do in word or deed, do all in the name of the Lord Jesus, giving thanks to God and the Father by Him.

Contents

List of Illustrations

Abbreviations

BN   Burlington Northern Railroad

C&S   Coeur d'Alene & Spokane Railway

CR&N   Coeur d'Alene Railway and Navigation Company

IN   Idaho Northern Railroad

NP   Northern Pacific Railroad

OR&N   Oregon Railway & Navigation Company

OWR&N   Oregon-Washington Railroad & Navigation Company

S&IE   Spokane & Inland Empire Railroad

SF&I   Spokane Falls & Idaho Railroad

UP   Union Pacific Railroad

W&I   Washington & Idaho Railroad

W&S   Wallace & Sunset Railroad

List of Maps

Foreword

THE STORY OF RAILROADING IN THE Coeur d'Alenes carries all the elements of a rousing novel set in a land of vast, rugged beauty. For those acquainted with Colorado's famous railroads, the story is strangely familiar: narrow gauge, dual gauge, and standard gauge track; small engines straining up steep grades and screeching across spindly trestles to conquer a high mountain pass; railroad wars, train robberies, high-jackings, and the courage of brave men risking their lives for others. The catalyst uniting all these elements was the fever of the big strike.

Unique on the list of big strikes was that of the Coeur d'Alenes. The Coeur d'Alene strike started like so many others with Andrew J. Prichard's discovery of gold on the north fork of the Coeur d'Alene River in 1883 and gained momentum when Noah Kellogg and Phil O'Rourke discovered the silver and lead of the great Bunker Hill claim on the South Fork in September 1885. But unlike the others it has carried on, and on, right to this present day! With a total production of over $4 billion worth of metal and shafts reaching 8,300 feet below the surface, the Coeur d'Alenes are indeed unique in the mining world.

In the beginning the Coeur d'Alenes posed an isolation and remoteness that threatened to break the excitement with a realization that lack of transportation would turn this bonanza into an unprofitable nightmare.

Into this vacuum stepped D. C. Corbin with a good eye for the quickest way to solve the problem. In 1886 he sent the narrow gauge rails of the Coeur d'Alene Railway & Navigation Company (CR&N) winding up the Coeur d'Alene River and following the South Fork to Wallace. This railroad was connected with the outside world by the use of steamboats across Coeur d'Alene Lake to Coeur d'Alene City where a branch line was built to the Northern Pacific (NP) main line.

With year-around transportation secured, the mines boomed, but this auspicious beginning soon became obsolete with the arrivals of the unbroken standard gauge line of the Washington & Idaho Railroad (W&I) and the NP's own standard gauge line from Montana.

As this scene of mines and the railroads that served them evolved from the 1880s, we can be thankful that some of the saga has been captured and kept alive through photographs. The work of many photographers is presented in these pages; however, special recognition must be given to three, for without their efforts this book would not have been possible.

The first two were responsible for a collection of over 200,000 negatives now known as the Barnard-Stockbridge Collection. This collection was the product

Photographer T. N. Barnard, family, and friends at the Barnard home in Wallace, Idaho.

of Mr. T. N. Barnard and his business associate Miss Nellie Stockbridge who together operated the Barnard Studio in Wallace, Idaho.

Thomas Nathan Barnard, the founder of the studio, started his photographic training in 1880 at the age of 19 under a relative, Mr. Laton A. Hoffman, who operated a photographic studio in Miles City, Montana Territory. After working and learning three years, Barnard made a number of moves in the West ultimately bringing himself and his wife of two years to Wallace in 1890.

Barnard's first studio in Wallace was started just in time to be destroyed by the 1890 fire that wiped out the town, but both the town and the studio were quickly rebuilt. The new studio prospered with the town and brought in so much business that Barnard contacted a relative who was a photographer in Chicago and asked her to join the business. It was thus that Miss Nellie Stockbridge came to Wallace in 1898.

The two photographers proceeded to take pictures of every phase of life in the booming mining town. Miss Stockbridge learned from Barnard as they packed their 50-pound camera, glass

The Barnard Building in 1907 was the home of the Barnard Studio (lower left). It also housed the J. C. Penney Company with its "Golden Rule" sign proclaiming "175 busy stores."

plate negatives, and developing material around the mountains taking scenic views.

In the summer of 1915, ill health caused Barnard to move to Spokane, Washington. While wintering in Los Angeles in February, 1916, he died of typhoid fever at the age of 55. The studio was left in the hands of Nellie Stockbridge who carried the operation on past her ninetieth birthday. In April of 1965 Miss Stockbridge died in Wallace at the age of 97.

The year before her death the Barnard-Stockbridge Collection was donated to the University of Idaho Library. The collection included over 200,000 nitrocellulose and glass plate negatives. The staff of the library has had the monumental task of organizing the collection and transfering the negatives to less dangerous and more durable forms. In addition to portraits and scenic views of towns and mines, railfans of today can be thankful that the collection also contains photographs of locomotives, trains, trestles, and stations.

Other fine railroad pictures are the work of the third photographer instrumental in this book, Mr. Ronald V. Nixon of Polson, Montana. Mr. Nixon has a collection of about 30,000 photographs, the majority of which are connected with railroads. He took his first photograph, the crew of a circus special,

Barnard-Stockbridge Collection
University of Idaho Library
Miss Nellie Stockbridge, shown here on a 1946 trip to Missoula, began a partnership with T. N. Barnard starting in 1898. Due to Barnard's illness in 1915 Miss Stockbridge started running the studio without his help. She carried on this work even at the age of 90.

when he was five years old. Both his father and mother held jobs with the NP in Montana, so it was natural for him to have an interest in railroads from his early childhood. The young Nixon's first job with the railroad was telegrapher for the NP at Livingston, Montana. After working for other various companies in this same capacity, he took a position in 1929 with the Canadian Pacific Railway in Calgary, Alberta, but by 1930 he was back in Montana working as a telegrapher for the NP again. In addition to this job, he also spent five years dispatching trains and several years as chief rules examiner at Minneapolis railroad school. Throughout his career

R.V. Nixon Collection
Ronald V. Nixon in the cab of Northern Pacific number 1356, the ten-wheel veteran of the Coeur d'Alene branch. This photograph was taken in Missoula, Montana, on October 16, 1955, where this engine is now on display.

with railroads, Nixon has been active as a railroad photographer and historian.

In 1930 Nixon's first published photograph appeared in the *Railway Age*. Since that time his work has appeared in magazines such as *Railroad, Trains,* and *Modern Railroads*. He has also written numerous railroad articles for newspapers and magazines, and his photographs have been enjoyed on posters for the Milwaukee Road, the Great Northern, the Soo Line, Electro Motive, General Electric, and the American Locomotive Company. Ronald Nixon's work has left the modern railfan a rich heritage that is beyond price.

Through the work of these three photographers and numerous others it is still possible to view a panorama of the historic *Railroads through the Coeur d'Alenes*. But today the railroads that serve the Coeur d'Alenes bear little resemblance to the tiny narrow gauge line started in 1886 or its standard gauge successors — gone are the narrow gauge and its steamboats, gone are the steam engines, gone is the "S" bridge landmark of the NP standard gauge, and now even the NP branch line itself has been abandoned by the BN — yet still we can relive that glorious time when the Coeur d'Alenes were in their heyday.

R. V. Nixon Collection

Ronald V. Nixon caught in action photographing Northern Pacific No. 3 near Eddy, Montana (east of Thompson Falls), on July 2, 1952. Ron is using his old standby, a 4 x 5 Speed Graphic.

Acknowledgments

GIVING PROPER CREDIT TO ALL WHO aided in the preparation of this book is certainly a large task, but far larger were the hearts of those that shared their time and resources to help preserve the history of this area. Time and again complete strangers willingly gave of themselves, and many are now close friends. This inspiration kept this project moving, and to all I am greatfully indebted. Following is a list of the individuals and organizations that helped through answering letters, supplying information, and providing photographs:

George B. Abdill, James Bening, Ch. (Col.) H. G. Benton, H. L. Broadbelt, Mike Denuty, John R. Fahey, Gene Foster, Henry R. Griffiths, Ross Hall, Dr. Philip R. Hastings, Cornelius W. Hauck, Philip Johnson, Marvin L. Jones, Michael Koch, Frank Kyper, John T. Labbe, Richard Magnuson, Julian Marshall, Warren R. McGee, Clyde Parent, P. E. Percy, Bill Pike, Bert Russell, L. P. Schrenk, L. E. Shawver, Robert Wayne Smith, Bert Ward, Charles Weart, and C. R. Wilburn.

Donald Springer and Mrs. Driscole, Coeur d'Alene District Mining Museum; Eleanor M. Gehres, Western History Department, Denver Public Library; Mrs. William M. Kelly, Eastern Washington State Historical Society; Jim Davis, Idaho State Historical Society; Theodore Holloway, Inland Empire Railway Historical Society; Mrs. Glenn Strombo, Mineral County Museum and Historical Society; Mrs. Ruby J. Shields, Division of Archives and Manuscripts, Minnesota Historical Society; Rex Meyers and Lori Morrow, Montana Historical Society; Carl G. Krueger, Museum of North Idaho; Janice Warden and Elizabeth Winroth, Oregon Historical Society; Charles A. Webbert and Lois Ackaret, Department of Special Collections and Archives, University of Idaho Library; Raymond Wilson, University of Idaho Photo Center; Raymond W. Karr, Region 1, USDA Forest Service; the Photo Library, U.S. Geological Survey; and John F. Guido, Department of Manuscripts, Archives, and Special Collections, Washington State University.

In addition to these, a very special thanks must be given to Bob Lowry, John Kennaugh, Ron Nixon, Bob Pearson, and Maynard Rickerd for the many hours they have spent in research.

Finally, I acknowledge the support of my wife, Linda, for without her encouragement and assistance, this book would never have progressed beyond the stage of dreaming.

Thank you all.

RAILROADS THROUGH THE COEUR D'ALENES

Chapter One

The Opening Scene

IN THE NARROW PANHANDLE OF NORTH Idaho along the western border of Montana lies the area referred to as the Coeur d'Alene Mining District. It constitutes the lands drained by the Coeur d'Alene River system and is generally divided into the areas of the North and South Fork districts.* The river system is one of two that feed the waters of Coeur d'Alene Lake; the other being that of the St. Joe River. The Coeur d'Alene system drains the west side of the Bitter Root Mountains which form the boundary between Idaho and Montana. In the early days this northern extension of the Bitter Roots was often referred to as the Coeur d'Alene Mountains.

In April of 1842 when Father Pierre Jean DeSmet made the earliest recorded visit of a white man to the area, he named the present Coeur d'Alene River the St. Ignatius. After teaching the Coeur d'Alene Indians, Father DeSmet promised to build a mission for them. The promise was fulfilled in the fall of 1842 when Father Nicholas Point and

F. J. Haynes Foundation Collection
Montana Historical Society

The Cataldo (or "Old") Mission and a group of Coeur d'Alene Indians in the year 1884. Construction of this building had been initiated in 1848 by Father Anthony Ravalli, and it was opened in 1852 or 1853. At the time of this photograph the start of the narrow gauge railroad was still several years in the future. When work on it began in 1886, the first rails were laid at the "Mission" station. (The site of the station is believed to be at the bottom of the small hill the Cataldo Mission rests upon. This would be behind the building in this photograph.)

Brother Huet built the Sacred Heart Mission of logs near the mouth of the St. Joseph (St. Joe) River. Annual flooding at this site prompted Father Anthony Ravalli to begin a new structure in 1848 on the Coeur d'Alene River at the loca-

---

*Although the earliest records and maps use the term "North Fork Coeur d'Alene River" in referring to the main branch of the river which Prichard Creek feeds and which brought the early gold miners to the area, about 1910 USGS maps began using this term in reference to a smaller branch which joined the original "North Fork" at Linfor from the west. This smaller stream, which flowed past Bumblebee, was originally called the "Little North Fork." This new terminology now called the main branch which flowed from the northeast simply the "Coeur d'Alene River." As the old records (and most of the inhabitants of the area) use the original designation, this will be used throughout this book.

tion now known as Cataldo. This new structure was finally opened in 1852 or 1853. Today called the "Old Mission" or Cataldo Mission, it has been restored and attracts hundreds of visitors each year.

The year 1853 also occasioned the arrival of Isaac Stevens, Washington's Territorial governor, to the Coeur d'Alene Valley. Stevens and 240 men were making a government survey for a possible northern route of a transcontinental railroad. His subsequent report did recommend a route following the south fork of the Coeur d'Alene River; however, the first northern transcontinental railroad, the NP, instead chose to swing far north around Pend Oreille Lake to avoid crossing the imposing Bitter Root Mountains. (Interestingly, the later Coeur d'Alene Branch of the NP did follow Stevens' recommended route, and many in the area felt it should have become the main line.)

During the year of 1859, Captain John Mullan, formerly a lieutenant on Stevens' survey team, began to explore the route for a wagon road to connect Fort Benton, Montana Territory, with Fort Walla Walla, Washington Territory, under a Congressional appropriation of $30,000 for the survey and $230,000 for the actual construction. As with the Stevens' survey, Mullan avoided the Clark Fork River, the eventual route of the NP main line, because it was subject to periodic flooding and selected the route of the St. Regis and Coeur d'Alene rivers.

The actual construction of the 624-mile road was carried on with a 100-man crew beginning in 1860. After that, improvement work continued until halted in 1863 due to the Civil War. The route followed part of an old Hudson's Bay trail around the south end of Coeur d'Alene Lake, crossed the mouth of the St. Joe River, and continued to the Mission on the Coeur d'Alene River. An alternative route, which later became the main one, skirted the north side of Coeur d'Alene Lake, climbed over the Fourth of July Pass, and dropped down to the Mission. Heading eastward, the road ascended the South Fork until it was three miles east of the present town of Mullan, there turning south and climbing over Sohon's (or St. Regis) Pass, and then down the St. Regis-Deborgia River (the route of the Coeur d'Alene Branch of the NP to Missoula).

Although the Mullan Road was often in such bad condition that it stretched the truth to refer to it as a road, it did meet a desperate need for transportation in the area. This is clearly shown by the more than 20,000 people with their supplies who used the route in the year of 1866 alone. The end of the Montana gold rush of the 1860s brought a decrease of traffic and further deterioration of the road.

Strangely, the beautiful forested valleys of the north and south forks of the Coeur d'Alene River managed to hold their secret of vast mineral wealth as skilled miners tramped the Mullan Road on the way to and from strikes in Montana and further south in Idaho. Even early rumors of gold in the Coeur d'Alenes coming from the crew of Captain Mullan and others failed to prompt any action. Apparently the first documented prospecting in the area was done in 1878 by Thomas Irwin who located a claim near the Mullan Road. The following year, A. J. Prichard led a group north of the Mullan Road over the Evolution Trail and discovered Prichard Creek on the north fork of the Coeur d'Alene. A member of Prichard's group, Gellett, discovered placer gold on that

The Northern Pacific freight depot in Spokane Falls under construction in 1881. The NP line was built through this area just in time to serve the gold strike on the North Fork in the Coeur d'Alene mining district. Much of Spokane Falls' early prosperity was due to the Coeur d'Alenes.

Celebration at Spokane Falls September 9, 1883, for the first regular train from the east. The Northern Pacific depot displays a "welcome" sign as well as other lavish decorations.

THE NORTHERN PACIFIC RAILROAD

BEGINS AT ST. PAUL, MINNEAPOLIS AND DULUTH,

And runs through the Lake and Park Region of Minnesota, the Red River Valley, the Renowned Wheat Fields of North Dakota, the Weird Scenery of the Pyramid Park, the famous Yellowstone Valley, the Rich Grazing Fields and Mineral Districts of Montana, and the Extensive Forests and Mining Regions of Idaho.

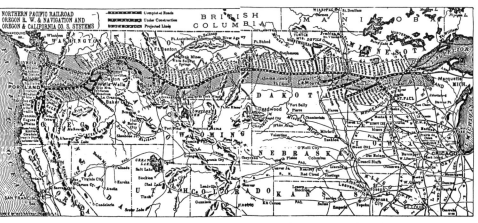

And is the ONLY Line running to the Yellowstone National Park; the ONLY Line running to the Districts of Agricultural and Mineral Wealth in Washington and Oregon; the ONLY Line running to Puget Sound, "The Mediterranean of the Pacific," and the ONLY Line running to British Columbia and Alaska.

THE ONLY LINE RUNNING TO

THE CELEBRATED GOLD FIELDS OF THE

COEUR D'ALENES.

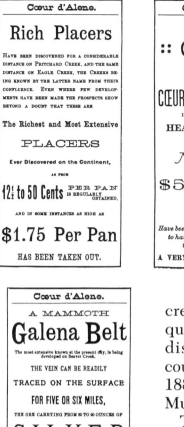

"In the Gold Fields of the Coeur d'Alenes" was a sensational pamphlet issued by the Northern Pacific Railway to popularize the Coeur d'Alene mining district and thus promote its own business.

creek in 1882. Prichard attempted to quietly leave the area and report the discovery to friends, but the secret could not be kept. The years of 1883 and 1884 marked a great gold rush in the Murray-Eagle area.

The newly completed NP — the gold spike having been driven September 8, 1883 — did all that it could to encourage the boom and thus increase its own traffic. To that end it issued a sensational pamphlet, "In the Gold Fields of the Coeur d'Alenes," making fantastic

Panning for gold at Scott's Placer in the Murray area in 1897. This area had already seen heavy operations as is evidenced by the extensive rock wall and flume. By this date the only really profitable gold operations here were hydraulic mining and dredging.

Barnard-Stockbridge Collection
University of Idaho Library

Hydraulic mining in Dream Gulch on the North Fork by the Spokane Hydraulic Mining Company. This shot was probably taken in the late 1890s. Earlier in the year 1890 the *Wallace Press* reported this company was using two "giants," one with a three-inch nozzle and one three and one-half inches discharging about 400 inches of water pressure that "is sufficient to send large boulders hurtling through the air when the body of water strikes them." The next year another giant with an eight-inch nozzle was to be put into operation! Today's ecology conscious generation would shudder at the devastation resulting from hydraulicing. Even in those days the *Wallace Press* of September 2, 1890, noted that "Someone has remarked that profitable placer mining requires the Missouri River for a head and all Hades for a dump."

F. J. Haynes Foundation Collection
Montana Historical Society

A number of early prospectors left the trains on the NP main line at Rathdrum, Idaho, then boarded a stage for Coeur d'Alene City on the way to the mines; but by the time of this photograph (April, 1887) the Spokane Falls & Idaho Railroad had been constructed from Hauser Junction to Coeur d'Alene (finished by the end of 1886) and much of the early excitement at Rathdrum began to die down. The first NP depot appears on the right and the water tank is at the far left.

claims of placers "unequaled in richness" and earnings of "$100 per man per day!" Although the railroad insisted they used great care in investigating these claims, "that they might not be accused of endeavoring to create a 'boom,'" the majority of those that answered the call found the good ground already taken and disgustedly left the area. Nevertheless, 18,220 ounces of gold were produced in the year 1885 alone by those that found good claims and stayed.

But the boom on the North Fork soon faded as easy riches disappeared. Events were rapidly leading to a different kind of bonanza to the south. The year 1884 saw the location of lead-silver claims on the South Fork that would far eclipse the importance of gold on the North Fork. There were the Ore-or-no-go, Tiger, Poorman, Black Bear, San

R. V. Nixon Collection

This picture shows NP engine No. 101, a 4-4-0 which was later numbered 742, at Rathdrum in 1888. The interesting sign behind the engine reads "railroad crossing." The end of the depot appears on the right.

Poling a dugout, or bateaux, up the North Fork. In the early days this was one of the primary means of moving freight up to Eagle City from the Mission. The charge was twenty-five cents a pound. This picture was taken in 1897 one mile up the North Fork from its mouth.

Francisco, and Gem of the Mountains claims on Canyon Creek; the Polaris in Polaris Gulch; and the Gold Hunter, Morning, and You Like claims near Mullan.

The most famous of all the South Fork discoveries was made in 1885 when Phil O'Rourke and Noah Kellogg located the Bunker Hill claim, followed by the location of the Sullivan claim by "Con" Sullivan and Jacob Goetz. Now the vast potential of the South Fork was beginning to present itself. The year 1886 signaled a major rush to the South Fork as the North Fork continued to wane.

Transportation to both of these areas had presented a major problem right from the first. The most apparent route in the beginning was the old Mullan Road, but neglect and annual flooding made it nearly impassable. New routes needed to be found. Generally the traffic funneled through either Coeur d'Alene City to the west or Thompson Falls to the east.

The traffic coming through Coeur d'Alene City reached that point by leaving the NP main line at Rathdrum and by walking or taking a stage. At the lake the government steamboat *Amelia*

Wheaton, soon joined by other steamers, carried the fortune seekers across the lake and up the Coeur d'Alene River as far as the Mission in low water or Kingston in high water. Travelers bound for Eagle or Murray could leave the steamer and pay to be poled up the North Fork in a dugout or hire a packtrain up the South Fork to Jackass Creek

Beaver Station was about halfway between Wallace and Murray on the Nine Mile Road. The road opened in 1888 and this photograph was taken on August 8, 1898. Beaver Station was not only a well-known stopping place for travelers, but was also the site of many social functions. The first building, also known as Red's Place, burned to the ground on January 1, 1889. It was rebuilt as this two-story building about 25 feet by 60 feet which opened February 14, 1889.

"The Sunset Route" stage between Wallace and Murray ran daily over the Nine Mile Road starting in December of 1888. Shown here the stage is leaving Murray with a load of passengers "up top." The group is either sitting out posing for the camera, or perhaps trying to escape the heavy dust that plagued travelers in the summer.

and then over the Jackass Trail to the gold fields. To aid travel from Coeur d'Alene City, two enterprising merchants of that town, Clement King and James Monaghan, constructed a rough road from the Old Mission to Murray. Travelers bound for the South Fork claims traveled from the Mission up the Mullan Road. The difficulty of this is graphically illustrated by the adventure Colonel Wallace had bringing his wife from the Old Mission to the town of Wallace, which he had founded. This trip which covered only 25 miles took two days and required the fording of the threatening high water of the South Fork 14 times! Fortunately the only casualty was a drowned chicken.

Heavy traffic forced some improve-

Thompson Falls, Montana Territory, on the NP main line in 1884 was serving its second year as the jumping off point for prospectors heading to the Coeur d'Alenes from the east. This photograph by F. J. Haynes, then the official NP photographer, is one of a number taken to popularize the area — and the railroad.

ments for travelers heading east of the Mission. In 1886 stages ran three times a week between there and Wardner, and the Two Mile Road was built connecting Osburn and Delta. The following year stages ran between Wallace and Mullan, operated by G. W. Marsh, and between Wallace and Osburn, operated by Billy Haskins. The latter was forced to halt in October when the road again became impassable. The year 1887 also marked the commencement of work on the Nine Mile Road connecting Murray and Wallace. Donations of $595 by public spirited Wallace citizens made the start possible. The road was finally finished in November 1888, and a daily stage, the "Sunset Route," was begun in December.

Even after the railroad had reached the area, these trails and roads remained important avenues of trade. When traffic was halted over Coeur d'Alene Lake by the breakdown of the icebreaker *Kootenai* in early 1888, freight and mail were again carried by packtrains from Coeur d'Alene City over the Mullan Road to the mines.

Even more important than the transportation routes from Coeur d'Alene City (in terms of supplying Eagle, Murray, and Burke) were the connections with Thompson Falls in Montana Territory. While the NP first stopped at Belknap and advertised it as the jumping off point for the Coeur d'Alenes, the citizens of Thompson Falls forced trains to stop at their town and convinced the miners and the railroad that they had the deserving community. An old Indian trail connecting Thompson Falls and the mining area became the basis for Thompson Falls Trail. The trail began at Thompson Falls and followed Prospect Creek for miles, swung right to cross Thompson Pass at an elevation of 4,859

feet, then dropped down to Murray and Eagle. Another route left Prospect Creek and swung left over Glidden Pass at an elevation of 5,768 feet, then descended to Burke. Until the railroad arrived this was the main traffic route to and from Burke, since the much shorter distance to Wallace did not receive a road until after the railroad had been completed! The Thompson Falls Trail was soon converted to a rough wagon road — taxes were levied in March, 1885, to build the road from Thompson Falls to the Idaho border. In addition to the Thompson Falls Trail, the less used Belknap and Trout Creek trails also crossed into Montana to connect with the railroad.

Traveling the Thompson Falls Road in 1887 was a dangerous business. On August fifth E. J. Catleff, a freighter headed for Thompson Falls, was relieved at gunpoint of $135 by three men on Glidden Summit. The men were never caught. On August fourteenth three other men were robbed by a lone gunman between Murray and Thompson Falls. John Hachett lost $500, a watch, and a ring. C. W. O'Neill lost $40, a gold watch, and $2,000 belonging to the Bank of Murray. Although a large reward was offered, this crime was never solved.

In addition to the threat of bandits, travel on these early roads was marked by narrow escapes from forest fires and runaway wagons. It is no wonder that mine owners sought a safer, cheaper method of transportation.

The Bunker Hill and Sullivan mines shipped their ore by wagon to the Old Mission in 1886. From there it crossed the lake by boat to Coeur d'Alene City and was shipped to the smelter in Wickes, Montana. The Tiger Mine in Burke was shipping ore to Thompson

Freighting by wagon between Murray, Idaho, and Thompson Falls, Montana, became one of the primary methods of supplying the North Fork camps following the opening of the wagon road between these two points. Taxes to build this road were first levied in Missoula County, Montana, in March of 1885. This early photograph shows the first freight line preparing to leave Murray. G. B. Williams, the owner, and his son John occupy the first wagon, followed by other drivers Alvah Sumner and Frank Sumner. The mud in the street and the blanket around John Williams testify to the difficulties of travel during this period.

Falls and then to the smelter. Much of this early ore was shipped without any concentration, a very expensive operation. Something had to be done.

The year 1886 saw no less than six plans to build railroads in the Coeur d'Alenes! J. C. Davenport planned a 14-mile horse tram from the Mission to the mines. Stephen Glidden, Noah Armstrong, C. W. Turner, and others from Montana were planning a railroad. J. J. Browne of Spokane organized the Spokane & Coeur d'Alene Railroad to build a line connecting the NP main line with Coeur d'Alene City and another line from the Mission to the mines on the South Fork. Browne tried to get the support of the NP as did Anthony M. Cannon, president of the Spokane & Palouse Railroad, who had a line surveyed south of Coeur d'Alene Lake and up to the mines. The fifth company involved in planning was headed by D. C. Corbin, and the last was the Washington & Idaho (W&I) backed by the Oregon Railway & Navigation Company (OR&N).

Chapter Two

The Entering Wedge

THE RACE WAS ON! SIX DIFFERENT schemes to tap the wealth of the Coeur d'Alenes — which would be first?

J. J. Browne's plan to build a standard gauge branch from the NP main line to Coeur d'Alene City, and this connected by steamboat with a narrow gauge line up the Coeur d'Alene River to Wallace, showed the most promise for rapid construction. Not only did the use of steamboats cut down on the number of miles of track to be laid, but also the plan of using narrow gauge would require a less substantial roadbed than standard gauge, thus saving additional time and money. But Browne had a mistaken notion that Congressional approval to build the railroad was necessary, therefore causing his plan a fatal delay. While he was struggling in Washington, D.C., Daniel C. Corbin, a young entrepreneur from Montana, was able to woo the indispensable support of the NP. This spelled the doom for all other plans except that of the W&I with its backing of the OR&N.

Corbin incorporated his Coeur d'Alene Railway & Navigaton Company (CR&N) on April 22, 1886, and the papers were filed in the Territory of Montana several months later. Listed as incorporators were D. C. Corbin, Sam T. Hauser, A. M. Holter, Anton Esler, S. S. Glidden, James Wardner, and James Monaghan. The articles spelled out two major routes for the line. The first was to originate at or near Thompson Falls "running westerly or southerly to the south fork of the Coeur d'Alene River, thence down the south fork and Coeur d'Alene River to the Old Mission." The second route was to run "from the town of Coeur d'Alene northwesterly to Rathdrum, or such point on the Northern Pacific, with the right to run a

Daniel Chase Corbin, the man who opened the Coeur d'Alenes through construction of the SF&I and the CR&N.

Marvin Jones Collection

The first train to Coeur d'Alene City in 1886 appears in this heavily retouched photograph. This railroad, the Spokane Falls and Idaho, was constructed using engine No. 3 (a 4-4-0) of the Spokane and Palouse.

branch of extension in southerly direction from Shoshone to Nez Perce County." If this plan seems familiar this is because it is practically a carbon copy of the plan J. J. Browne proposed!

The failure of the articles to mention possible branches in the mining area would later prove to be a huge headache when the NP took over, but for now they had more pressing business. In

July of 1886 the NP directors agreed to work on the standard gauge portion of the line from the NP main line to Coeur d'Alene City.

(To more easily understand what happened, the three aspects of Corbin's plans will be taken separately. The chronology in the appendix shows the three concurrently.)

The Spokane Falls & Idaho Railroad

This standard gauge portion of Corbin's plan was first called the Spokane & Idaho, but later the name was changed to Spokane Falls & Idaho (SF&I) when the line was completed and finally incorporated in the state of Washington.

July of 1886 saw the start of surveying and grading, although a formal contract with the NP was not signed until the middle of August. Tracklaying began on October fourth and was finished by the twenty-fourth. The chosen route left the NP main line at Hauser Junction, seven miles west of Rathdrum, and passed through Post Falls on the way to Coeur d'Alene City for a total length of about 13.5 miles. By the end of 1886 the line was in the hands of the operators as the

Idaho Historical Society

The Northern Pacific ore dock appears in this early picture taken from Tubb's hill. The date was the late 1880s, shortly after the SF&I was turned over to the NP. Up the railroad to the right is a two-stall engine house with twin smoke jacks (building partly hidden by a tree). Further up the road to the right is the depot (also partly hidden).

Museum of North Idaho

The Northern Pacific train would back down to the Coeur d'Alene ore dock to load freight passengers from the mining area as this picture shows ca. 1890.

Eastern Washington State Historical Society

The first excursion to Coeur d'Alene City on the Spokane Falls and Idaho used the Spokane and Palouse engine number three which was also used for the SF&I construction. This picture was taken near Coeur d'Alene.

F. J. Haynes Foundation Collection
Montana Historical Society

Hauser Junction (where the SF&I or Ft. Sherman Branch diverged from the NP main line to Coeur d'Alene City) was the site of this beautiful winter picture taken by Haynes in March of 1891. NP engine No. 121 (a 4-4-0) heads the "F. L. Down's Special" to Coeur d'Alene. The last car of the train is Haynes Palace Studio car. Windows in its center section appear to extend up and over the top of the car possibly forming one of the earliest "dome" cars.

Donovan Photo
Museum of North Idaho

This Northern Pacific 4-4-0, No. 121, displayed the white flags of an extra as it posed in Coeur d'Alene City ca. 1890s.

Eastern Washington State Historical Society
Fort Sherman Branch train in the Spokane valley headed from Coeur d'Alene City to Spokane Falls about 1900. This section was on the NP main line.

last piece, the dock in Coeur d'Alene City, was finished.

The SF&I never had any equipment of its own and was built using a Spokane & Palouse engine and NP cars. The NP formally leased the SF&I on October 1, 1887, and it later became known as the Fort Sherman Branch. (The name Fort Sherman was used to distinguish this line from the Coeur d'Alene Branch which was built from Missoula to Wallace. Fort Sherman was the U.S. Army post at Coeur d'Alene City.)

In the early years, operation on this branch centered around the ore traffic from the Coeur d'Alene Mining District. In the evening the ore boats arrived at

S.& I.E.	S.& I.E.	309 Ex Su	307 Ex.Su.	FORT SHERMAN BRANCH	308 Ex.Su.	310 Ex Su	S.& I.E.	S.& I.E.
11 05	5 45	3 00	6 30	208 Lv...Coeur d'Alene...Ar	12 35	6 45	8 45	3 15
......	......	3 18	6 48	217 ....Post Falls........	12 09	6 22	......	......
......	......	f3 23	f 6 53	219 ......Grand Jct.........	f12 06	f6 16	......	......
......	......	3 30	7 00	221 ....Hauser.........	12 01	6 10	......	......
......	......	3 42	7 12	........Otis Orchards.......	11 45	5 58	......	......
12 20	7 00	4 15	7 45	242 Ar........Spokane....Lv	11 15	5 30	7 30	2 00

Fort Sherman Branch timetable (NP) dated August 1, 1917. The S&IE listed was the Spokane & Inland Empire electric line service.

Photo by Kroemer
Marvin Jones Collection

The Northern Pacific depot in Coeur d'Alene as it appeared ca. 1917 when the Idaho National Guard, Company C, left for the First World War. This brick depot is probably the third one built (earlier ones were destroyed by fire). Today it still stands though used as a restaurant.

the NP dock at the foot of Third Street in Coeur d'Alene. A large group of men transferred the ore by hand to the waiting standard gauge cars. The next morning the train would leave for Spokane Falls. The return train would reach Coeur d'Alene City in the early afternoon. On the edge of town, the train would run around a wye track, then back over a mile down to the dock. The schedule forced travelers from the mining area to spend the night in Coeur d'Alene, an unhappy prospect for them since most were headed for Spokane. Around the turn of the century, the schedule was changed so that the trains left Coeur d'Alene in the late afternoon and returned the next morning. Both these schedules annoyed the citizens of Coeur d'Alene since taking care of any business in Spokane required spending the night there.

For almost twenty years travelers to and from Coeur d'Alene had no choice of railroads since the NP branch was the only line. This changed in 1903 when the Coeur d'Alene & Spokane electric line built into town. Eventually four different lines served this community. For a short time the NP scheduled two passenger trains a day to Coeur d'Alene to fight for booming passenger excursion business on the lake, but the automobile soon brought an end to this bonanza.

Today much of the old branch line is torn up. The dock and wye are gone, and more track is scheduled for abandonment. The Burlington Northern (BN), successor of the NP, now operates into Coeur d'Alene on the electric line

Barnard-Stockbridge Collection
University of Idaho Library

The ore hauler *Coeur d'Alene*, here moored at the NP dock, was purchased by D. C. Corbin and used by the Coeur d'Alene Railroad and Navigation Company to haul much of the ore between Mission and Coeur d'Alene City. Its superstructure was later placed on the *Georgie Oakes*.

trackage it acquired from the Great Northern, and the NP depot has been turned into a restaurant.

Steamboats

Corbin arranged the waterborne portion of his transportation system on July 31, 1886, by contracting with the Coeur d'Alene Steam Navigation & Transportation Company. This organization operated the stern-wheeler *Coeur d'Alene* and the smaller propeller-driven *General Sherman* (the second steamer on the lake) between Coeur d'Alene City and the Mission. Both boats had been built to handle the traffic during the gold rush days on the North Fork. This contract was only temporary, for the CR&N purchased the Coeur d'Alene Steam Navigation & Transportation Company in the spring of 1887 thus making secure this link in the system.

Over the years the fleet of the CR&N was increased and improved. The first addition was the icebreaker *Kootenai*, built by the Willamette Iron Works in the fall of 1887 and launched on December eleventh. The *Kootenai* with its iron hull was absolutely necessary to keep the ice of the lake broken and the ore moving during the winter months. This was clearly shown in January of 1888 when a breakdown of the *Kootenai* caused a 20-day blockage in the system. Tons of ore piled up which took months for the line to remove once it was reopened. To aid the movement of ore a new iron barge, given the flashy title *Barge No. 3* was launched in November of 1888. (No information is available on the first two barges which were probably purchased with the Coeur d'Alene Steam Navigation & Transportation Company.)

The most famous addition to the fleet was the *Georgie Oakes,* which came to

be the most popular steamer on the lake. While under lease to the NP, the CR&N contracted with a Portland ship builder to replace the hull and machinery of the old *Coeur d'Alene* and thus increase its capacity from 50 tons of ore to 100 tons. (The resulting boat carried only the superstructure and cabins of the *Coeur d'Alene* and the old hull was turned into another barge.) The *Georgie Oakes,* named for a daughter of NP president Thomas F. Oakes, was first steamed up in the spring of 1891. She made regular trips to the Mission until the end of 1896 when she was switched to a run that ended at Harrison and no longer connected with the CR&N narrow gauge at the Mission.

The NP sold the *Georgie Oakes* in 1908 after it was declared unsafe. The new owner, the Red Collar Line, rebuilt her at a cost of $10,000 and operated her until 1920. Her end came on the Fourth of July in 1927 when citizens of Coeur d'Alene made the unfortunate move of burning her as a patriotic gesture.

Long before this the rest of the NP-CR&N fleet had been sold. The competition of the OR&N (later the Union Pacific) forced the fleet, with the exception of the *Georgie Oakes,* into idleness by 1890. In 1891 H. Karsten and J. F. Stephens purchased the *General Sherman, Barge No. 3,* and the hull of the old *Coeur d'Alene.* The *Kootenai* was still used occasionally to

Minnesota Historical Society

Ornate letterhead used by the CR&N

Old Mission landing with engine No. 1 of the CR&N heading a mixed train. In the foreground a barge is being loaded with sacked ore. Behind is the steamer *Coeur d'Alene*.

break ice until 1898 when her machinery was removed and the hull sold.

The Coeur d'Alene Railway & Navigation Company

Actual contruction of the CR&N narrow gauge was begun by William L. Spaulding on August 18, 1886, under a contract for grading and construction signed on August ninth. The grading was finished during October, and track-laying with 40-pound steel rail laid to three-foot gauge began on November first. Work was halted on December twenty-sixth not far from the mouth of Milo Gulch and the site that would be Wardner Junction. (This was on the north side of the river across from what is now Kellogg.) All had not gone well between Spaulding and the CR&N. He brought legal action against the CR&N the next spring for moneys claimed. The

CR&N stock certificate number 501 issued to D. C. Corbin.

Kingston in 1893 looking downriver toward the Mission five miles distant. The CR&N track appears on the left as well as a very small building at track height (about the middle of the picture) which was probably the depot.

case lingered in the courts until 1896 when Spaulding won a judgment for $23,675 plus interest and costs. Further work on the railroad was left to others.

The first two locomotives were brought across the lake by steamboat near the end of the year 1886. They were operated for about a week before chinooks (warm winds) thawed the black loam roadbed, thus putting an end to operations since the time had not been taken to ballast the track. One engine was left between Pine Flat and Mud Prairie, and the other between Kingston and the Mission.

With the arrival of spring in 1887, the track was repaired and ballast applied. On March twentieth operation to Wardner Junction was begun. The Bunker Hill purchased ground at the Junction to stockpile ore, but for some reason

waited until October to begin hauling ore there. The right-of-way was cleared to Wallace by July, and along the way the town of Osburn (then called Georgetown) was laid out. The first train reached Osburn on August twenty-second.

The destination of the line was Wallace, Idaho, then a thriving town of about 500 persons which occupied the central location at the eastern end of the mining district. This was reached on September 10, 1887, as the narrow gauge rails were laid into town. The town realized the importance of this event and planned its first big celebration.

On Friday, September thirtieth, a train arrived carrying a large crowd including a sizable delegation from Wardner. The weather did not cooperate, and

Wardner Junction at Milo Gulch. Across the river is Wardner. The CR&N depot, a boxcar, and wye track appear in the foreground.

the program was marred by rain. (Many future celebrations would have the same bad luck.) Col. W. R. Wallace, the master of ceremonies, gave a "neat speech" according to the *Wallace Free Press* (October first) in which he accurately predicted that, "Now with the advantages of steam and rail we promise you a city of ten-thousand souls, with all the comforts the same implies." He was followed by the Honorable Albert Hagan who referred to D. C. Corbin in his address as "a little man from Montana." After some music Fred Dubois and Adam Aulbach spoke.

That evening a ball was held in the new Carter Hotel, and a song composed for the occasion by Mrs. X. S. Burke was sung. The chorus captured the crowd with the words, "To the railway and engine whose coming we bless, may thy length still increase, may thy power ne'er grow less."

The celebration was hardly over before the first of many legal actions brought operations grinding to a halt. The W&I had managed to survey their line through Wallace ahead of the CR&N, and during construction the narrow gauge line failed to follow its own survey through town, instead building on the north side of the river which was claimed by the W&I.

The injunction held up operations on 1½ miles of track until October twenty-ninth when Judge Buck dissolved it. This allowed regular train service to finally begin on November second. It was rumored that the CR&N (backed by the NP) paid $60,000 to settle the dispute, but if this was true — there was no confirmation — even that was not the end of the matter but only the beginning of a series of legal battles with the W&I.

Wallace became the scene of bustling railroad activity. The 24 x 80-foot depot there had been enclosed by this time, but it was not completed until November twelfth. Plans were also made to build a four-stall roundhouse in the vicinity of the wye track at the eastern end of town. (One leg of the wye formed the beginning of the Canyon Creek Railroad, the history of which appears in Chapter Five.) While this four-stall roundhouse was never built, a two-stall engine house was finished in December of 1887. Train service included a mixed westbound which left Wallace at 9 A.M. and an eastbound which arrived at 2:30 P.M. In December of 1887 the third locomotive was acquired. This made it possible to improve service and relieve some employees from extremely long hours. The *Wallace Free Press* of December tenth described the new service, "Engine number 3 in charge of conductor Flynn lays over nights here instead of returning to Junction. Engine number 2 is now used for pulling ore from the Junction to Mission. Until a few days ago conductor Flynn and his crew have returned to the Junction after coming to Wallace in the afternoon and hauled ore down to Mission, making very long hours."

Passenger rates from Wallace were 50 cents to Osburn, one dollar to Wardner, two dollars to Kingston, two dollars and 50 cents to Mission, and five dollars and 50 cents to Coeur d'Alene City. When the Canyon Creek Railroad was opened in December, the passenger fare from Wallace to Burke was 50 cents one way.

Freight rates were 85 cents per hundred pounds between Coeur d'Alene City and Burke, 80 cents per hundred between Coeur d'Alene City and Wallace, and 10 cents per hundred Wallace to Burke. The following year, 1888, rates from Coeur d'Alene were as follows:

Coeur d'Alene to Portland	$10.40 per ton
Coeur d'Alene to Tacoma	10.40 per ton
Coeur d'Alene to San Francisco	13.40 per ton
Coeur d'Alene to Omaha	17.00 per ton
Coeur d'Alene to Newark, N.J.	21.60 per ton
Coeur d'Alene to Wickes, Mont.	5.00 per ton

Although the distance to Wickes, Montana, was less than that to the other loca-

Barnard-Stockbridge Collection
University of Idaho Library

The Wallace depot and town as of 1888. At this time only the CR&N line existed with a passing track. Hidden behind the depot is a train, and just above the depot appears a very interesting rectangular water tank that is enclosed for protection from the cold.

CR&N engine No. 2 at Wallace (could be just starting up Canyon Creek Branch) decorated for the Fourth of July. The popular engineer Levi Hutton is on the far right. Behind the flatcar converted for the occasion is one of two homemade cabooses. The standard gauge track in the foreground belongs to the OR&N.

tions, the rate was still disproportionately lower than the rest. The fact that Corbin and others connected with the NP had an interest in the smelter at Wickes could explain the situation. Over the years the city of Portland especially came to resent what they considered excessively high rates of the NP from Coeur d'Alene mines. Later when the NP and UP began to battle over the control of the OR&N, it was largely the opposition of Portland that cost the NP control of that line.

This business which Portland coveted was growing rapidly. By the spring of 1888 the narrow gauge was unable to handle all the business, and it was necessary to purchase 20 new freight cars to keep shipments from being delayed.

At this time the narrow gauge rails extended 25 miles from the Mission to Wallace with the seven-mile branch from Wallace to Burke. This was to be the greatest extent of the line as an independent company under Corbin's control. For the NP, which viewed this area as within its domain, was fearfully watching as the W&I (backed by the OR&N) advanced into the Coeur d'Alenes. The NP made the decision to take over control of the CR&N, but even before this could take place it hired men through Corbin's company (June 30, 1888) in an apparent attempt to draw laborers away from the W&I construction crews.

On September 14, 1888, the CR&N was leased to the NP for 999 years. The NP did not assume control until October first, so in the meantime the old owners ran the line for all it was worth. The steamer *Coeur d'Alene* made two round trips a day, and the *General Sherman* worked with a barge. The railroad kept three trains running, and according to the *Wallace Free Press* "a wonderful amount of ore can be moved every day."

Operations on the line during this time reflected the rough nature of the mining camps it served. An incident which occurred shortly after the NP took over, recorded in November 17, 1888, *Wallace Free Press*, gives a humorous account of those wild times.

Conductor Ed Brown — How He and His Brakemen Done Up a Gang of Thugs

About a dozen or 15 men crowded into the up caboose of the freight train Wednesday evening at Mission to come up here [Wallace] to work on the grade between here and Mullan. They were full of poor whiskey and were in consequence rough and boistrous. When Billy (the brakeman, we could not learn his other name) was handing out the rear lights prepatory [sic] to leaving Mission, he was pushed off the car by these ruffians and otherwise interfered with. Conductor (Ed) Brown finally succeeded in pacifying the crowd and the train pulled out. They had made Kingston, climbed the hill and were flying down the east grade when the toughs evidently concluded to take charge of the train. Ed Brown was alone, the brakeman being on the outside. He endeavored to quiet the gang by mild means, but failed, and when one of them became unrulable [sic] and extremely insulting in his language, Ed planted him a right hander, which silenced him until the battle was over. This opened the ball [game] and Brown had the fun of seeing four of them fall before they overpowered him. At that juncture Billy appeared and lost no time in letting them know of his presence. He was doing great work when one of the ruffians hit him in the back of the head with a bottle. This knocked him senseless and soon the crowd subsided. Brown was not hurt, but as soon as Billy came to he asked, "What s-- of a b---- hit me with that bottle?" A great big six footer responded in the affirmative and had no sooner done so than Billy had him down on the floor, fast putting an end to him. Brown finally pulled him off. When the train stopped at Wardner Junction, Billy assisted his antagonist off the car by a gentle blow and proceeded to finish the job on the depot platform, but was finally pulled off again. Several of the roughs were put off the train bodily at the Junction and the rest came on to Wallace in quiet.

As the newspapers usually portrayed railroad men "bigger than real life" and as heroes, it is no wonder that generations of boys grew up envying their position. Also noticeable was the way the newspapers stressed self-reliance. To take matters into their own hands without waiting for the representatives of law and order, was as common for railroad companies as for individuals. This would soon be clear as the NP and W&I were now drawing lines for battle.

Now that the NP had taken over, D. C. Corbin was no longer part of the scene. Since the opening of the CR&N, Corbin had run the line at a great profit for himself and other investors. Time would show that he had sold at just the right moment, for fortune would soon change for the little narrow gauge line.

The part the CR&N played in opening the Coeur d'Alenes was not forgotten. In 1890 the Governor of Idaho, George L. Shoup, remembered the line as "the entering wedge which opened the marvelous treasure of the Coeur d'Alene to the world."

Chapter Three

The Challenge

OF ALL THE PLANS FOR BUILDING RAIL-roads into the Coeur d'Alenes, the one with the easiest grade and ultimately the most successful was the Washington and Idaho Railroad (W&I). This line applied for incorporation in Whitman County, Washington Territory, July 3, 1886, three days before the CR&N filed in Montana! The incorporators were George W. Truax, Horace F. Stratton, Julius Galland, Isaac Cooper, and Warren Sayre. The stated purpose of the company was to build a railroad and telegraph line from Farmington to

Eastern Washington State Historical Society

This magnificent structure, opened on April 20, 1890, was Spokane's first Union Station. It served the OR&N and the Seattle, Lake Shore and Eastern Railroad (later sold to the NP) until 1904 when the building burned.

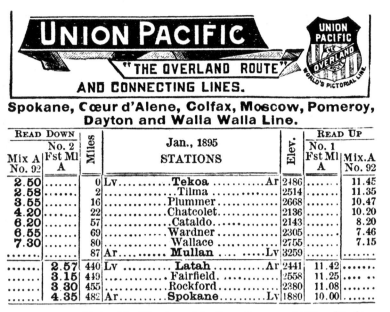

UNION PACIFIC
"THE OVERLAND ROUTE"
AND CONNECTING LINES.

UNION PACIFIC — WORLD'S PICTORIAL LINE

Spokane, Cœur d'Alene, Colfax, Moscow, Pomeroy, Dayton and Walla Walla Line.

READ DOWN			Jan., 1895			READ UP	
Mix A No. 92	No. 2 Fst Ml A	Miles	STATIONS	Elev.	No. 1 Fst Ml A	Mix.A No. 92	
2.50	......	0	Lv............Tekoa............Ar	2486	......	11.45	
2.58	......	2	............Tilma...............	2514	......	11.35	
3.55	......	16	..........Plummer..........	2668	......	10.47	
4.20	......	22	.........Chatcolet.........	2136	......	10.20	
6.20	......	57	..........Cataldo..........	2143	......	8.20	
6.55	......	69	.........Wardner..........	2305	......	7.46	
7.30	......	80	.........Wallace..........	2755	......	7.15	
......	......	87	Ar.......Mullan.........Lv	3259	......	......	
......	2.57	440	Lv.........Latah.........Ar	2441	11.42	......	
......	3.15	449	.........Fairfield...........	2558	11.25	......	
......	3.30	455	.........Rockford..........	2380	11.08	......	
......	4.35	482	Ar.........Spokane.........Lv	1880	10.00	......	

Union Pacific timetable from January, 1895, edited to show only service between Spokane and Wallace. Note that while Mullan is shown, no service is listed (track from Mullan to Wallace was abandoned the previous year). Also no passenger service to Burke is shown.

Eastern Washington State Historical Society

Spokane's Spanish tiled second Union Station was opened May 4, 1906. In addition to serving the OR&N (later called the OWR&N) it also handled the Idaho & Washington Northern. One of the ornate I&WN passenger cars appears behind the station.

Spokane Falls (both in Washington Territory), and to build a branch line along Hangman Creek across the Coeur d'Alene Indian Reservation to Wardner, Idaho Territory. Rights to operate steamboats on Coeur d'Alene Lake were also given.

This charter was accepted on July 12, 1886, and at the first meeting George W. Truax was elected president, a post he held until August 24, 1891, when Sidney Dillon, the Union Pacific president took over. While the W&I was to connect with a proposed OR&N line at Farmington (an OR&N branch from Colfax to Farmington was ordered constructed on May 21, 1886), the W&I apparently began life independent of the more powerful OR&N — at least on paper.

A survey was rapidly pushed into the Coeur d'Alene Mining Area with most of it, such as the location through Wallace, predating that of the CR&N. Before the end of 1886 the survey was completed.

Work on the line then became slow or nonexistent until the UP leased the OR&N on April 25, 1887. Soon the mining area was to become the battleground between the UP and NP giants.

The "war" began on a strange note as both combatants began operations by proxy. The NP started to treat the CR&N as its own, although it didn't legally assume control until October 1, 1888. Likewise the UP, through the OR&N began to run the W&I, although legal ownership wasn't transferred until May, 1888. In this strange climate the W&I began to extend UP influence into an area the NP considered its exclusive domain. The OR&N had crews in the mining area in September of 1887, and through the W&I it enjoined the CR&N from operating over 1½ miles of the nar-

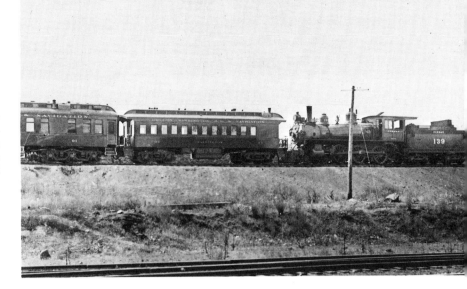

This 4-6-0 OWR&N engine No. 139 was photographed in the Spokane yards with the interesting open vestibule coach "Washington" and the much larger closed vestibule car "Oregon" (on the left).

row gauge track laid on the W&I survey through Wallace.

This injunction was dissolved in October and the OR&N men were withdrawn from the area as the UP and NP opened talks about a joint lease of the OR&N. While agreement was finally reached and ratified by all three lines in January of 1888, by March an injunction restrained the executing of the joint lease. Three directors of the OR&N from Portland, infuriated over the high NP shipping rates to their city, thus caused the war to resume. Other events of this spring were also destined to bring great change to the Coeur d'Alene country.

From the beginning the major obstacle to construction of the W&I had been the 53-mile crossing of the Coeur d'Alene Indian Reservation. Federal approval was necessary for construction, and the W&I fight for it was an excellent example of the trials of "red tape."

On February 2, 1888, a bill was introduced by Senator Dolph to give the right-of-way through the reservation, and this passed the next month. May eighteenth the bill became law. While it appeared the battle had been won, this was only the beginning. Disagreements with the Indians held up the right-of-way until November ninth, but these

were worked out and the Secretary of the Interior approved a map of the definite location of the line on December 7, 1888. Seemingly *now* everything was ready. Then the Attorney-General of the United States submitted the opinion that the Secretary of the Interior has no authority to permit construction until the fixing of the actual amount of compensation. (This opinion was probably sought by NP interests.) *Finally* in February of 1889, a whole year after the bill was introduced, permission was again

This early OR&N two-car passenger train approaching Chatcolet, Idaho, is headed east to the mining district. The locomotive appears to be one of the OR&N "Rome" engines — probably a 4-4-0.

Clyde Parent Collection
Courtesy of Maynard Rikerd

A Chatcolet excursion on the OWR&N was the occasion of this five-car passenger train. Beyond the station is the water tank, and to the left is Lake Chatcolet.

Clyde Parent Collection
Courtesy of Maynard Rikerd

Looking east just beyond the Chatcolet Station shows the same train approaching the swing bridge across the St. Joe River.

Mike Denuty Collection

An early OR&N westbound passenger train approaching the Chatcolet swing bridge.

received from the Secretary of the Interior to build across the reservation.

During this struggle for the right-of-way the OR&N pressed on with work on both ends of the line outside the reservation. In May of 1888 two companies of engineers were sent to make new surveys of the line, and later in this month the W&I was formally leased to the OR&N. Up until this point little or no actual construction had taken place, but now work was pushed in earnest with grading starting June first at Farmington. Kilpatrick Bros. & Collins of Beatrice, Nebraska, had taken the contract to build the 140 miles to the mines. (Later there were other various companies that apparently received subcontracts.) In addition to the grading at Farmington work was also carried on on the eastern end beyond the reservation.

In another attempt to stop the OR&N the NP hired many men to work near Kingston ostensibly to improve the original alignment of the CR&N narrow gauge line, and to build the line on to

Coeur d'Alene City. Since little work was actually done, it appears that the real motive was to hire men away from the OR&N, and to build up manpower in case of a fight. The NP also used the area near Kingston against the OR&N by applying in Spokane Falls for an injunction to keep the OR&N from crossing the CR&N track at that location.

In other action for the NP, Brayton Ives and other stockholders of the OR&N sympathetic to the NP, brought suit in Supreme Court in New York to stop the OR&N officers and directors from building to the Coeur d'Alene mines and other projects encroaching on

Robert Pearson Collection
The swing bridge across the St. Joe River appears just beyond this early OR&N two-car passenger train. The locomotive (apparently a "Rome" 4-4-0) is headed west toward Spokane.

Museum of North Idaho
The original swing bridge was constructed in 1889 across the St. Joe River at Chatcolet. Here the bridge is in the open position to allow the *Georgie Oakes* to pass heading up river. The date was sometime after 1908 when she was sold to the Red Collar Line and rebuilt. The swing bridge itself was later rebuilt in 1921 at a cost of $136,800. It still serves the railroad to this day. Lake Chatcolet lies to the left in this photograph, and the rail line to the right leads to the Coeur d'Alene Mining Area.

The first regular OR&N train through Harrison is shown here in 1889 with the *Amelia Wheaton* (first steamer on Coeur d'Alene Lake) standing off the shore on the left. The smaller steamer on the far right is the *General Sherman* which was owned by the NP. To reach Harrison from Chatcolet trains crossed the St. Joe River on the swing bridge and headed north along the bank of Coeur d'Alene Lake about eight miles to Harrison, which is at the mouth of the Coeur d'Alene River (to the right in this photograph).

"NP territory." This was claimed to be a violation of the lease made in April, 1887, to the Oregon Short Line and UP. Justice Van Brunt granted a temporary injunction restraining the company from building.

This didn't appear to have much influence on the OR&N as work continued at an even greater pace. J. H. Smith of Portland was granted a contract and had nearly 700 men at work clearing outside the reservation. This was nearly done by the end of August, 1888. With this obvious violation of the injunction, the judge reconsidered in September and decided he had no right to restrain continuation of the work.

With many plans now being considered, the OR&N filed supplemental articles of incorporation for the W&I. (This kept the OR&N out of some legal difficulties that later plagued the NP concerning the incorporation of the CR&N.) These supplemental articles allowed construction of the following lines:

Farmington to Spokane Falls; from a point on this line near the forks of Hangman Creek, northerly across the Coeur d'Alene Reservation to a point on Coeur d'Alene Lake, and to the Coeur d'Alene River, easterly to the Coeur d'Alene Mission and thence southeasterly along the south fork of the Coeur d'Alene River to Wardner; from near Spangle northeasterly to a point on Coeur d'Alene Lake, about 5 miles north of the mouth of the Coeur d'Alene River; From the town of Milo, Idaho, along the south fork of the Coeur d'Alene River to the town of Mullan, Idaho; from Mullan, easterly across the Bitter Root Mountains to Missoula, Montana; from Endicott, Washington Territory, northeasterly, to a connection with the line from Farmington to Spokane Falls, at a point about 12 miles north of Farmington; from a point near the junction of the north and south forks of the Coeur d'Alene River, thence along the north fork and Pritchard Creek up said creek to the town of Murray, Idaho, with a branch from a point near the mouth of Beaver Creek up said creek to its source; and from the mouth of Nine Mile Creek, in a northerly direction along said creek to its source.

These ambitious plans revealed the real intentions of the UP-OR&N in the area, for although the lines from Spangle to Coeur d'Alene Lake, up Nine Mile Creek, and from Mullan to Missoula were never built; this last proposal to build to Missoula showed that the UP intended to carry the battle right into the heart of "NP territory."

As the year 1888 came to an end, the OR&N pushed completion of its grading outside the reservation; and although relations between the OR&N and NP were still terrible, an interesting "joint" effort appeared. J. H. Smith of Portland, who had a grading contract for the W&I, was also able to win the low bid on the NP extension of the CR&N from Wallace to Mullan. Thus, the same contractor and crew (over 400 men) were soon working on the two different railroads that often amounted to a single grade and double track due to the narrow canyon. However, before the year could end another injunction stopping construction by the OR&N was declared in New York, this time by Justice Patterson of the Supreme Court. Unlike the previous injunction, this one caused an end of work, although contractors claimed it was due to bad winter weather.

When the spring of 1889 arrived it was one of high hope for the OR&N. Final permission to build across the reservation had been received and W. T. Watson, location engineer, had run the survey from Mullan 125 miles east to Missoula, Montana. The previous year 34 miles of track from Farmington to Rockford had been laid, and construction was now under way to Spokane. (The first train would reach there on October 8, 1889.) Now the remaining 87 miles, Rockford to Mullan, would be rushed to completion.

Over 2,000 men were soon laboring, and by the end of August tracklaying had crossed the reservation and was halted at the St. Joe River awaiting construction of a swingbridge by Hoffman and Bates of Portland. Before the iron bridge could be finished, a temporary wooden bridge was thrown across the river in September allowing trains to continue work on the far side.

Not all construction that fall was carried on without incident. The NP, having failed to stop the OR&N in the courts, soon resorted to other means. The following incident reported in the *Wallace Free Press* of October 5, 1889 (later called "The Battle in the Clouds"), described the W&I entry into Wallace.

A Railroad War — Collision Between the NP and OR&N Forces

On Thursday morning the Washington & Idaho had a large force of graders, principally Italians, at the upper bluff to commence work on

Museum of North Idaho

The OR&N railroad facilities at Harrison were crowded between the town and the shore of Coeur d'Alene Lake. To the right of the water tank was the pump house, and on the tank's left was the passenger depot (built in 1892 — 40 x 60 feet). Beyond the depot was the freight house. The steamer is the *Georgie Oakes* as rebuilt in 1908 by the Red Collar Line. This dates the photograph as later than 1900. Harrison had become the largest town in Kootenai County by 1900 with a population of 702. Coeur d'Alene City had only 508 people.

Harrison, Idaho about 1900

Mike Denuty Collection

Snowy view of the new Harrison depot. The old depot and water tank appear across the tracks toward the lake on the left.

Museum of North Idaho

This westbound OR&N passenger train is passing the Grant Lumber Company just up the Coeur d'Alene River from Harrison. The date was about 1916, and surprisingly the locomotive appears to be one of the OR&N's old "Rome" 4-4-0's built in the 1880s or 1890s. This large sawmill was just one of many at this time which made Harrison the largest town in the county. Many of the mills supplied timbers for the mines.

the excavations at daylight. This movement was evidently anticipated by the Northern Pacific people, for they also had a large force on hand under Mr. Burnham, of Aldridge & Burnham, contractors on the railroad up Canyon Creek. Mr. Burnham's force, at the sight of the enemy with picks and shovels, set his small army up the mountain, and in a few moments it seemed as if pandemonium had broken loose. The side of the precipitous bluff was covered with a mass of laborers, yelling, shouting, and cursing, while the railroad track below was covered with a dense force of Washington & Idaho forces, apparently in possession of the right of way. Pretty soon, however, there was a racket as if an earthquake had shaken the hill, immense boulders came tumbling down, crashing and tearing through everything. There was a yell of rage from those below, and such an inglorious route [*sic*] was never before seen since the Mormons whipped the United States Army under Gen. Albert Sidney Johnston in 1857 at Echo Canyon, Utah. The Washington & Idaho graders fled in every direction to avoid the tons of rock that were hurled down upon them, and strange to say, no one was killed. The Washington & Idaho force was withdrawn and in one hour afterwards the Washington & Idaho served an injunction on the Northern Pacific representatives, and the fight was taken where it belongs — into the courts. There is going to be a hot legal contest for about one mile of this right of way.

The resulting legal decision by Judge Logan found that the OR&N could build through Wallace on the ground left beside the CR&N track, and the CR&N could keep its present track although it was built on the original W&I survey. Now the way was clear for the OR&N entry into Wallace.

As the year came to an end anticipation for the approaching railroad rose in all the towns along the line. Wardner was reached November nineteenth, and on December sixth the whistle of the "Big Iron Horse" was heard for the first time in Wallace. On the ninth the W&I finally entered Wallace in a terrible snowstorm. A spontaneous celebration composed of several hundred people and the Wallace Silver Cornet Band greeted the new line. Important person-

Idaho Historical Society

Springston ca. 1900 was a station stop on the OR&N less than four miles up the Coeur d'Alene River from Harrison. In the early days the railroad tried unsuccessfully to rename it Anderson. The small station is the last major building along the track to the left (about the center of the photograph). On the far right is the Springston Lumber Company's general store.

ages were contractor J. H. Smith, locomotive engineer T. H. Hill, and conductor W. H. Butterfield.

The first round trip from Wallace to Spokane Falls was made on December twenty-third. The journey one way took about six hours and fifteen minutes and

Idaho Historical Society

The OR&N roadbed between Harrison and Cataldo required a tremendous amount of fill as the valley was low and often flooded. This postcard view was taken looking east toward the mining area.

cost $6.50. The *Wallace Free Press* reported the only bad part of the trip was the dinner stop in Tekoa on the return where ". . . the meal served up on Monday night is not such a one as would draw a person to the same house twice. The butter was vilely rank, the biscuits like cobblestones, the coffee made from corn husks roasted and the cold meats tougher than the kids who grow up without parental restraint." For those willing to endure the trip following this glowing description of the food, regular departure from Wallace was scheduled at 6:15 A.M. with arrival in Spokane at 12:25 P.M. The return trip left Spokane at 4:00 P.M. and reached Wallace at 10:15 P.M.

The continuation of tracklaying from Wallace to Mullan was now put off until next year, but work continued on improving the facilities at Wallace. Earlier in September of 1889 twenty acres had been purchased one-half mile below the town for a roundhouse and machine shop. Since Wallace was to be a division point, the last major stop before crossing the divide into Montana, the facilities were to be extensive. The plans were to keep five engines in Wallace for local work.

Notwithstanding these great plans, operations were forced to begin on a modest scale. W. H. Burridge, local agent for the OR&N, had H. W. Williams, the ticket and express agent, set up office in a boxcar opposite the CR&N depot. A 20 x 68-foot passenger depot as well as a 20 x 40-foot freight room were soon under construction. These were located further east than the CR&N depot at the site of the current UP depot. Before the depot could be finished a more urgent task was to construct a 60-foot steel turntable. This project was completed on New Year's Eve of 1889. The

Idaho Historical Society

This early sawmill near Cataldo was one of the early industries along the OR&N. The rail line appears just behind the buildings. This photograph dated ca. 1900 shows the mill not long before it burned.

first locomotive was turned easily and the table pronounced the largest and finest between Wallace and Portland. Likewise, when the depot was finished and turned over to the operating department the following March, it was described as one of the handsomest structures on the line. (This didn't speak too well for the other structures as photographs reveal the depot was quite plain.) The roundhouse which was not completed until the fall of 1890, was originally constructed as a four-stall frame building — not as magnificent as expected — but the people of Wallace still had high hopes for the line.

Other operations of the OR&N in the

Hutton Collection
Eastern Washington State Historical Society

This interesting oxteam and logging wagon at Cataldo draws interest away from the very plain OR&N depot behind it. The depot building appears to be nothing more than a simple house with a station sign. Cataldo is twenty-seven miles above Harrison.

Barnard-Stockbridge Collection
University of Idaho Library

The Empire State-Idaho Mill (concentrator) at Sweeny was quite new in this ca. 1900 photograph. Sweeny, later called Bradley, was about ten miles above Cataldo and only about two miles below Wardner-Kellogg. The locomotive on the trestle is OR&N No. 160, a Rome 2-8-0 built in 1888.

spring of 1889 were a real encouragement. The track was finished from Wallace to Mullan by the end of March, and earlier that month McLane and Janse Contractors advertised for 200 men to begin work on a 6,800-foot OR&N tunnel, the longest of two tunnels that were to carry the line under the Bitter Root Mountains and into Montana. The entrance of the large tunnel was eight miles east of Mullan, and its completion was expected to take two years.

Although some digging was done, the project never really got off the ground. The reason for the sudden change of plans was not given locally, but later a high UP official who defected to the NP revealed the reason. His comments to the NP are contained in the next chapter, but the story from the UP point of view is as follows:

In 1888 Charles Adams, UP president, concluded that war with the NP was inevitable. A letter he wrote to R. S. Grant the following year clearly shows his feelings.

Barnard-Stockbridge Collection
University of Idaho Library

The Bunker Hill and Sullivan Smelter, just below Wardner-Kellogg on the OWR&N line, was not built until July 1917, but soon became a major industry. The plant is shown here on May 18, 1925.

Barnard-Stockbridge Collection
University of Idaho Library

The Bunker Hill and Sullivan operated various mills. This view shows the South Mill in 1907. Its operation was discontinued in 1912 as newer mills opened. Note the huge amount of cord wood in the foreground which was apparently still burned for power. On the right beyond the NP boxcars is the ore-house, and beyond it to the left the concentrator.

Barnard-Stockbridge Collection
University of Idaho Library

A "new" Kellogg passenger station appears in this 1907 view along with a freight building to its right, which is probably the original passenger station demoted in use. To the left of the passenger station is a work train repairing damage to a stream crossing.

. . . every letter I receive from my people at the West asseverates before the high Heaven that they are as pure as angels, and that their garments are unsullied as the driven snow, but that human flesh and blood cannot endure the long accumulation of wrongs which has been inflicted upon them by the demons of the NP.

One of Adams strategies for the war was to have the OR&N line from the Coeur d'Alene Mining Area extend from Mullan to Missoula, Montana, then on to connect with the Utah & Northern near Butte. The brilliant part of the scheme was to connect these lines with James J. Hill's Great Northern line which was then building toward the West Coast. In this way the UP would have a transcontinental line right through the "NP territory!" At least such was the plan.

Fortunes changed fast in this era and this was no exception. The UP plans were forestalled when the NP started construction of its own line from Missoula to Mullan (their Coeur d'Alene Branch). Since this was built largely on the OR&N survey, the OR&N was able to get an injunction stopping construction in the winter of 1889, but in the long run they were unable to stop the NP. If this was not enough to halt the

Don Roberts Collection
Oregon Historical Society

OR&N 2-8-0 No. 161, a Rome product built in 1889, was captured on film on this cold day before the turn of the century near Wallace. In 1901 it was sold to the Idaho Northern Railroad and would be operated between Enaville and Murray as their No. 2. The locomotive returned to the parent company in 1911 when the Idaho Northern was absorbed.

OR&N plans, the financial condition of the UP by the end of 1890 forced Sidney Dillon, then president, to quietly stop all construction possible. Thus died a plan that could have brought a transcontinental line through the Coeur d'Alenes; but the UP was not the only railroad with such ideas.

Business for the OR&N became brisk regardless of the failure to extend the line. As the OR&N had an "all rail" route, it enjoyed a tremendous advantage over the CR&N which needed to bag all the ore it shipped, transfer the ore from narrow gauge cars to steamboat at the Mission, then again transfer the ore from the steamboat to standard gauge NP cars at Coeur d'Alene City.

Idaho Historical Society

OWR&N locomotive No. 132 heads this passenger train through Osburn four miles south of Wallace. The mail car is picking up mail "on the fly" from the stand in the center of the photograph. The speed of the train blurs the image in this once common scene which has now passed into history.

Just south of Wallace this large six-car OR&N passenger train approaches town.

The NP also knew this and was thus building its own "all rail" route from Montana. But in the meantime the OR&N was able to steal the lion's share of the business from the CR&N. The increased traffic called for more trains, and a schedule for 1890 showed an express arriving from Spokane at 9:30 P.M. and leaving for Spokane at 7:00 A.M. The freight left for Tekoa at 8:55 A.M. and arrived from Tekoa at 10:35 A.M. By the next year business had grown so much that the new agent, Newell, was told to enlarge the freight depot in Wallace.

During this time of growth the OR&N planned, or threatened, to build numerous short branches in the mining area. This time the OR&N used the NP surveys to amend its articles of incorporation to allow construction up the canyons the NP had earlier located, much to the displeasure of the NP! The only one of these lines seeing actual con-

The Pioneer Sampling Works was constructed in 1890 a mile and a half below Wallace (up the canyon to the right in this photograph). The main building was 100 feet by 40 feet. The purpose of the company was to provide an independent assay of ore which was accepted by the smelters. This service was performed for a charge of 75 cents per ton. The company's official name was the Northern Sampling and Reduction Company. While it was originally constructed to handle 300 tons a day and employ 20 men, an 1892 report said it handled only 200 tons and employed 12 men. Over the years ore from the Gem, Standard, Poorman, Tiger, Mammoth, Black Bear, Custer, Hecla, Argentine, Golden Chest, Stemwinder, and Sierra Nevada mines were sampled there. The near side of the building was served by the OR&N standard gauge. A UP boxcar and a very interesting one of the Union Pacific Lincoln and Colorado appear in view. The far side was served by the CR&N narrow gauge. The end of CR&N boxcar No. 18 appears on the left.

Idaho Historical Society

This OR&N passenger train at speed is heading west just below Wallace during the 1899 mining war. The tent at right is part of the encampment of U.S. soldiers sent to stop the violence. The railroads played a part in the war as they transported the soldiers to the area.

struction at this time was from Wallace up Canyon Creek to Burke. This line is discussed in Chapter Five.

Another interesting sideline during this booming time was the OR&N's use of steamboats on Coeur d'Alene Lake. Although the "all rail" route of the OR&N was a great advantage, unfortunately the line was quite long and circuitous. Thus the line offered steamboat connections between Coeur d'Alene City and Harrison using the *Volunteer*, and in 1892 the People's Transportation Company was organized to do the job.

They also built the *St. Joe* in 1893 for this work.

By the spring of 1893 the OR&N (UP) operations had grown considerably. The following description was contained in the *Coeur d'Alene Miner* of February 25, 1893.

Our Railroads

To George A. Newell, agent of the Union Pacific, we are indebted for some scraps of information regarding the interests and business of that corporation in Wallace. The Union Pacific has a round house of four stalls. Contiguous to this is a coal bunker of 300 tons capacity, so arranged that the engines can be quickly

Don Roberts Collection
Oregon Historical Society

OR&N No. 164 posing with the proud crew at the original OR&N roundhouse in Wallace. This structure was built in 1890 and lasted until about 1909.

The OR&N Wallace depot appears in the foreground.
The date of 1889 is probably incorrect as the depot
wasn't finished until the spring of 1890. Nevertheless,
the date is soon after this. The narrow gauge track of
the CR&N shows in the foreground to the right of the
OR&N standard gauge line.

filled on either side by chutes. The water tank,
sixteen feet in depth, is filled from a spring on
the mountain side, and is always kept full by an
automatic feed. The stock yard is in a dilapidated condition and the agent hopes it will be
shortly repaired.

The road has eight sidetracks in Wallace, aggregating 7524 feet in length with a capacity of
275 cars, and track scales of sixty tons capacity.
It also has convenient facilities for transferring
freight and loading cars with the Northern
Pacific.

There are two main line passenger trains daily
and two freights, also an up and a down passenger on the Burke branch. In addition to the
crews of these men there are three crews of section men operating from this point. One of these
divisions extends to Burke, one to Mullan and
one to Osburn. The force of section men aggre-
gates from twelve to fifteen men, the number
being variable. The payroll amounts to about

By 1907 Wallace had grown to this large size. The original OR&N depot was still in use at the lower right, and the
OR&N roundhouse and coal dock can be seen on the upper right.

Picking up railroad express shipments for delivery was once a common activity at passenger depots. Here American Express wagons are loading an interesting assortment of freight at the back of the OWR&N depot in Wallace.

$2500 per month for the men stationed at this place.

Unfortunately the year 1893 and the "great panic" brought hard times for the mines, railroads, and the whole community, not to mention the rest of the nation. The price of silver and lead fell and the mine owners closed most of the mines as the mine workers refused to take lower pay and the railroads refused to lower their rates. Banks closed their doors and hard times reigned. Railroad service was cut to a bare minimum. The OR&N stopped all passenger service thus throwing a small amount of business back to the CR&N. The following spring of 1894 another kind of disaster hit the OR&N. Heavy flooding in June

The Coeur d'Alene Foundry in Wallace started business in 1892, and became well known for the excellent mining equipment it produced. The business was located above Wallace near the "wye" branching up Canyon Creek. This photograph was taken some time after 1910 when the OWR&N replaced the OR&N.

destroyed much of the roadbed between Wallace and Mullan forcing that section to be abandoned. Financially this didn't have much effect, for already the previous fall (October 13, 1893) the parent UP had applied for receivership. The W&I construction had played a big part in this, for the main reason given for the financial trouble was the extensive mileage in silver producing states where production had steadily declined. The W&I itself was foreclosed by the Bay State Trust Company in Spokane for a $4,616,400 mortgage on September 20, 1895. In 1896 the line was sold to the reorganization committee of the OR&N.

From this time on changes in the railroad (other than branch line construction covered in Chapter Five) would be very few. The facilities in Wallace were one area that did see improvements.

The original depot in Wallace had become woefully inadequate and a new one was ordered built. Dates given for its construction vary, but the original

depot was still used as late as 1907. A photograph taken early in 1910 shows the new depot finished, but the old one is sitting in the street next to it. This indicates that the new one had recently been completed and the old one was still being moved to a new location.

This new depot (which could be described as interesting but hardly beautiful) was finished just in time to be gutted by the great 1910 fire which wiped out the whole east end of Wallace. (On the other hand the NP depot was not even touched!) Nevertheless the shell that remained was soon rebuilt. This depot remained un active use until the end of July 1980, when it was abandoned by the UP for smaller, more economical office space in town. The future of the building is in doubt, but some residents hope to acquire and restore it for historical purposes.

At the lower (west) end of Wallace another change in OR&N facilities had taken place. The four-stall wooden roundhouse constructed in 1890 no longer existed by 1909 (as revealed in photographs of that year). Apparently it either burned or was torn down to make way for a new one. By 1910 it was replaced with a brick roundhouse with five stalls and a machine shop. This would last until it was demolished in 1957.

The year 1910 also saw a major reorganization of the railroad. All subsidiaries of the UP in North Idaho were merged with the OR&N and then reorganized as the Oregon-Washington Railroad & Navigation Company (OWR&N). From this time on locomotives were lettered for the UP with only small initials OWR&N on the cab.

The Wallace Branch of the OWR&N had now settled into a stable pattern that it would keep for many years.

SPOKANE, WALLACE AND BURKE

Nos. 22-26 Daily	Nos. 13-24 Daily	Nos. 9-22-26 Daily	Miles	TABLE No. 17	Elevation	Nos. 21-10 Daily	Nos. 25-23-14 Daily	No. 21 Daily
......	3.05	8 35	0.0	Lv....SPOKANE......Ar.	1893	11.30	6.00	......
......	3.52	9.22	21.8	........Manito.........	2574	10.47	5 12	......
......	f 3.55	f 9.25	22 6	..........Bell..........	2526	f10.45	f 5.10	......
......	f......	f......	25 3	..........Hagen.........	2645	f......	f......	......
......	f......	f......	27.4	..........Weller........	2582	f......	f......	......
......	f 4.10	f 9.40	29.5	..........Ford.........	2445	f10.25	f 4.50	......
......	4.30	10 00	36.6	Ar....Amwaco.....Lv	2123	10.05	4.35	......
8.55	......		0 0	Lv....Tekoa......Ar	2472			12.20
9.10			7.0	........Lovell.........	2570			f11.55
9.25	Via	Via	12.2	........Watts.........	2938	Via	Via	f11.40
9.35	Steamer	Steamer	15 1	.......Plummer........	2651	Steamer	Steamer	11.25
f 9.55	Harrison	Harrison	22.6	......Chatcolet.......	2122	Harrison	Harrison,	10.55
f.......			26 1	........O'Gara........	2122			f........
10.25	5.05	10.25	30.3	Ar....Harrison......Lv	2122	9.30	4.10	10.25
10.25	5.05	10.25	42 6	Lv....Harrison......Ar	2122	9.30	4.10	9.30
10.45	f 5.30	10.45	46 1	......Springston.......	2122	9.15	3.55	f 9.15
f.......	f.......	f.......	50.3	......Black Lake......	2122	f.......	f.......	f.......
f11.00	f 5.45	f11.00	53.3	......Medimont.......	2124	f 9.00	f 3.40	f 9.00
11.10	5.55	11.10	57.3	........Lane.........	2123	8.50	3.30	8.50
11.20	6.05	11.20	61.4	......Rose Lake......	2123	8.40	3.20	8.40
11.30	6.15	11.30	63.1	........Dudley.......	2125	8.30	3.10	8.30
11.40	6.25	11.40	69 6	........Cataldo.......	2129	8.20	3.00	8.20
11.50	6.35	11.50	74 6	........Enaville.......	2158	8.10	2.50	8.10
f.......		f.......	76 2	......Pine Creek......	2177	f.......	f.......	f.......
			79 1	........Sweeney.......	2230	f.......		
12.15	6.50	12.15	81.3	...Kellogg-Wardner...	2291	7.55	2.35	7.55
f12.35	f 7.05	12.35	87 9	........Osborne.......	2518	f 7.40	f 2.20	f 7.40
1.00	7.25	1.00	92.3	Ar....WALLACE.....Lv	2731	7.30	2.10	7.30
1.00		1.00	92 3	Lv....WALLACE.....Ar	2731		2.00	......
f.......		f.......	96 1	........Gem.........	3245		f.......	......
f.......			96.5	........Frisco.......	3292		f.......	......
f.......			97.2	........Dorn.........	3401		f.......	......
f.......			97 9	........Mace.........	3518		f.......	......
1.30		1.30	99 0	Ar....Burke......Lv	3734		1.30	......

Trains 21, 22, 23 and 24 carry Parlor Car between Harrison and Wallace.
Trains 21 and 22 will stop on flag at Clark's (Chatcolet Bridge).
Trains 10 and 14 will stop at main line stations to discharge passengers from Wallace and Lake Creek Branches.

OWR&N timetable of January 20, 1917, including service through Amwaco and service between Wallace and Burke.

Chapter Four

The Challenge Accepted

When the NP assumed control of the CR&N on October 1, 1888, they knew they were in for a real battle with the UP (through the OR&N and W&I). Since the Coeur d'Alene Mining Area was within the area of land granted to the NP by Congress in its original charter, it is no wonder that they resented the approach of the rival line. In addition to filing various legal actions against the W&I as related in Chapter Three, the NP's plan called for construction of an "all rail" route to the mines. The NP realized that the CR&N narrow gauge could not survive against the W&I's "all rail" line, so it set out to build its own.

Two possible routes presented themselves. Track could be continued from the end of the CR&N line near Mission over Fourth of July Pass to Coeur d'Alene City. There a connection with the SF&I line (Ft. Sherman Branch) of the NP would be made. The other possibility would be to build along the line surveyed by the OR&N east from Wallace across the Bitter Roots to Missoula, there connecting with the NP main line. Along with these two plans was the option that both could be built with the finished line offering a shortened main line (cutting off the great bend in the old NP main line which went far north around Pend Oreille Lake).

The Fourth of July Pass Route

The old CR&N narrow gauge terminated on the west end at the Old Mission. The scheme of extending the line from there to Coeur d'Alene City and converting the rest to standard gauge was conceived by the NP before it acquired the line. Transferring the ore, as the current system required, was just too inefficient. Several routes between the Mission and Coeur d'Alene City were possible, but the most direct was from a point on the CR&N two miles above the Mission, up the Fourth of July Canyon to the summit, then down the drainage system to Coeur d'Alene Lake, and around the lake to Coeur d'Alene City.

Beginning in the fall of 1888 the NP put crews in the field surveying the 30-mile route, and before the end of the year reports were coming back that a maximum grade of two percent could be kept with a single tunnel not over 900 feet long.

The official report of the survey came the next spring in a report from H. S. Huson to J. W. Kendrick. "During the year surveys between Coeur d'Alene City and the Mission have been completed, and a line has been secured over the Fourth of July Summit upon a 116-foot maximum [2.2%], with 16-degree curves." Following this report the project seemed to stall.

One difficulty that surfaced in 1891 was the restrictive charter of the CR&N

which did not permit amendment for new lines. To get around this the proposed line was now called a branch of the SF&I (which currently terminated at Coeur d'Alene City). But regardless of what it was called, construction was never begun.

Many factors were probably responsible for the death of the project. The construction of the Coeur d'Alene Branch to Missoula put a financial strain on the NP. Economic conditions were deteriorating and so were the labor conditions in the mines. Finally, a period of truce with the rival OR&N allowed several joint agreements to be signed which eliminated the need for new duplicate construction.

Although construction of the line faded out of the picture of NP projects, it is interesting that several proposed railroads tried to resurrect it. In 1892 newspapers reported that a line called the Salt Lake, Seattle & Boise Railroad would build to the mines over Fourth of July Canyon during that summer. This was never done. Even more interesting was a line organized in 1914, the Spokane, Wallace & Interstate, which also planned to use the route, and reportedly let a contract for grading fifty miles between Coeur d'Alene and Wallace. This proposal also failed, Interstate 90 now runs over much of this route which the railroads never conquered.

The Coeur d'Alene Branch

Instead of constructing the line up Fourth of July Canyon, the decision was soon made to build from Missoula. One of the main factors in this was the hope that such a move would "spoil" the route as a new virgin territory for the UP. The risks of this plan were great as construction costs would run very high

in this rugged area, and the NP had never been in very good financial condition. But apparently the threat of the UP left no choice, for in the fall of 1889 the decision was made to begin construction. Even before this tentative moves had been made in this direction.

As the NP prepared to take over the CR&N in the fall of 1888 they assured the local communities that they would extend the narrow gauge road to Mullan, and on November 8, 1888, a contract for grading from Wallace to the Hunter concentrator just above Mullan was awarded to J. H. Smith. While the track was laid to three-foot gauge, the roadbed was constructed for standard gauge (which hinted at the future plans). The section to Mullan was finished in March with the first train reaching there on the twenty-fourth. This train was headed by locomotive No. 3 with engineer Al Matheson, fireman Fred Brewer, and conductor Tom Cosgrove greeting the cheering crowd. (It is interesting that the NP ignored the name Mullan and called their station "Ryan" after Dennis Ryan, owner of the Hunter Mine. But the name Ryan was never accepted by the community and soon disappeared, even from NP timetables.)

The construction from Mullan to the Hunter concentrator, just above town, was held up until June eighteenth by legal maneuvering of the OR&N. These efforts of the OR&N were against a joint agreement with the NP (this was set by a commission appointed by the courts to settle differences between the two lines). The tactics used by the OR&N caused an NP official to warn his superior in August of 1889 that "Our operations in the Coeur d'Alene country will undoubtedly bring on a war. It is necessary that our legal papers be perfect. We are fighting a wiley enemy. . . ."

Finally, notwithstanding OR&N opposition, contracts were signed by the Woods, Larson & Company on November nineteenth for construction between Missoula, Montana, and the Hunter concentrator. The 127-mile line was to be built from both ends. The section from the Hunter concentrator to the Idaho-Montana summit was built under the nominal ownership of the CR&N, and the section from the summit to Missoula under a line called the Northern Pacific and Montana.

This section on the Idaho side was apparently constructed as standard gauge although this precluded use of the CR&N trains for construction. However on the positive side, narrow gauge rails would only need to be widened about seven miles so standard gauge trains could reach Wallace once the rest was completed.

Tracklaying on the Montana side was begun in January, and by April over

thirty miles had been completed. One report claimed that over 2,000 men were at work and that a mile of road was being finished each day. By August the line was completed except for forty miles on the western end where considerable work was yet to be done.

This construction on the western end, with its crossing of the Bitter Root Mountains was a formidable challenge. From the beginning officials realized that it would be necessary to tunnel under the summit to keep the line at a reasonable grade and curvature. And just like the OR&N they made plans to do this tunneling. One reason the railroad town of Pottsville was built above Mullan was to prepare for this tunnel work, but this kind of work took much time.

To rush completion of the line the NP decided to build a "temporary" overhead line using four percent grades and curves of 16 degrees. The permanent line using the tunnel would have a maximum grade of only two and two-tenths

Eastern Washington State Historical Society
The first train between Wallace and Missoula stopped at Lookout Pass. This excursion took place on August 15, 1891. An earlier train had passed over the line in December of 1890, but it was only able to go as far as Mullan, since the track below there was still narrow gauge. The sign being held from the baggage car reads, "Sunset — Elevation 4,680 feet." This is quite confusing as a later branch up Nine Mile Canyon had a stop called "Sunset." Apparently the name Lookout Pass was not used until later. Nevertheless, there is no doubt that the location is Lookout as the sign marking the pass a few years later reads the exact same elevation.

percent and curves of 14 degrees. But as time would show the "temporary" line was the only line constructed, although plans to build the tunnel continued for years.

The actual pass the "temporary" line would use seemed difficult for the engineers to describe. In some reports it was called St. Regis Pass, some Sohon's Pass and others Mullan Pass. All these were incorrect, for St. Regis Pass (which was also called Sohon's Pass) was several miles to the west at the headwater of the St. Regis River, and Mullan Pass was further to the east at the headwater of the south fork of the Coeur d'Alene River. The actual pass used was apparently unnamed at that time as the name Lookout Pass did not appear until several years after work was begun.

Even though construction of the tunnel was "postponed," building over the summit was still far from easy. Several very large trestles were needed, one of these being the beautiful "S" bridge, and another a large trestle just below Dorsey, Idaho. In Montana other notable features on the line were two 150-foot and two 100-foot spans across the Missoula River (now called the Clark Fork), the Fish and Rock Creek trestles each over 100 feet high, and the 650-foot tunnel at Borax, Montana.

The rails from both sides were finally joined somewhere near the summit on December 22, 1890. The *Wallace Press* reported, "Miss Glidden, the daughter of S. S. Glidden, broke a bottle of wine or rather sent it over the precipice where the last spike was driven, and there was an all-rail route completed from Wallace to the Atlantic seaboard via the great Northern Pacific. . . ." A train of dignitaries from Missoula including the NP assistant civil engineer was delayed by two feet of new snow

and didn't arrive until the following day. This train was unable to run all the way to Wallace as the track below Mullan was still narrow gauge, so the party had to transfer for the ride to the big celebration that evening (December 23) at the Wallace pavillion.

An attempt to run a train from Mullan to Missoula on December twenty-seventh failed. Neither the "S" bridge nor the trestle at Dorsey were completed, so the earlier train had passed the "S" bridge by using a switchback and the other trestle by a temporary line. Now the snow was so deep that when the train was forced to run in reverse on the four percent grade after the switchback, it stalled and had to return to Mullan.

Although operations on the line were closed "temporarily," hopes for it were high and some went so far as to claim that it would soon become the new NP main line. While NP officials didn't voice this claim, they were nevertheless proud of the new branch line. They were especially proud of the effect its construction had on the OR&N. Earlier in August of 1889 J. W. Kendrick, chief civil engineer, reported to NP president T. F. Oakes:

Our business in this district has been badly cut by the Union Pacific Road, owing to the fact that with their broad gauge system the transfer of ores and merchandise was unnecessary, which gave them a considerable advantage, both with respect to time and waste in breakage. As soon as our line is completed from the east, we shall enjoy a correspondingly great advantage over the Union Pacific. In this connection, it may be of interest to you to state that Mr. G. J. Smith, formerly General Manager of the OR&N Division of the Union Pacific Road, told me recently that it had been fully arranged to have the Great Northern Road construct through Missoula to a connection with their system in the Coeur d'Alenes, and that the commencement of that construction by the NP had the effect of causing the Great Northern to adopt the northern route to the coast. As the earnings of the Missoula station now amount to over half a million dollars, annually, and as the consummation of this arrangement would have practically ruined our Coeur d'Alene Lines, and would furthermore have resulted in their building a line that they had already located, between Missoula and Garrison, thus giving them a through line from Portland to Butte, through our territory, it seems to me that the Company [NP] has every reason to congratulate itself upon the construction of the line to the Coeur d'Alenes. We are deriving considerable business from this branch, and new and valuable mineral discoveries are being made on the side of the Bitter Root mountains, in the streams tributary to the St. Regis river. With the business of the Coeur d'Alene district, and the new business that we shall derive at various points along this line, it will be a valuable branch.

While Kendrick was now able to engage in this self-congratulations, a few short years later he probably came to regret placing his name on this report. But for now the hopes were high and everyone was looking for great things from the new line.

Success was not yet at hand, however, for the natural elements had not been reckoned with. Not only did snow keep the line closed for the entire winter of 1890–1891, but when spring came it was discovered that the rock in the tunnel at Borax had swelled and had broken timbers in the roof for about 100 feet.

By the time this tunnel and other repairs were made the summer of 1891 was well underway. The first train to pass over the line this year reached Mullan on July twenty-seventh with a party of NP surveyors and officials including Superintendent Ramsey. While the track had now been widened to standard gauge back to Wallace, the train couldn't use it because the roadbed was not ready for the heavy engines.

In mid-August several excursions were run over the line to promote business between the mining area and Mon-

tana. The first of these left Wallace through a triumphal arch and ran to Missoula, returning the following day. The second excursion originated in Montana and brought businessmen to Wallace. As the line was about to be turned over to the operating department on August twenty-fifth, the *Wallace Press* took occasion to acclaim the new line:

The people of the Coeur d'Alene had looked longingly and lovingly for the approach of the iron horse from the East, across the huge divide, which stood threateningly as an insurmountable barrier to a closer relationship with our Montana brethren, and when the news flashed upon us that engineering skill had finally overcome all obstacles, and that the shackles of isolation had been removed, our people felt like a community released from bondage.

R. V. Nixon Collection

NP pile driver No. 9 is shown here working on the construction of the Coeur d'Alene Branch in 1890. The locomotive is a cap-stacked 4-4-0.

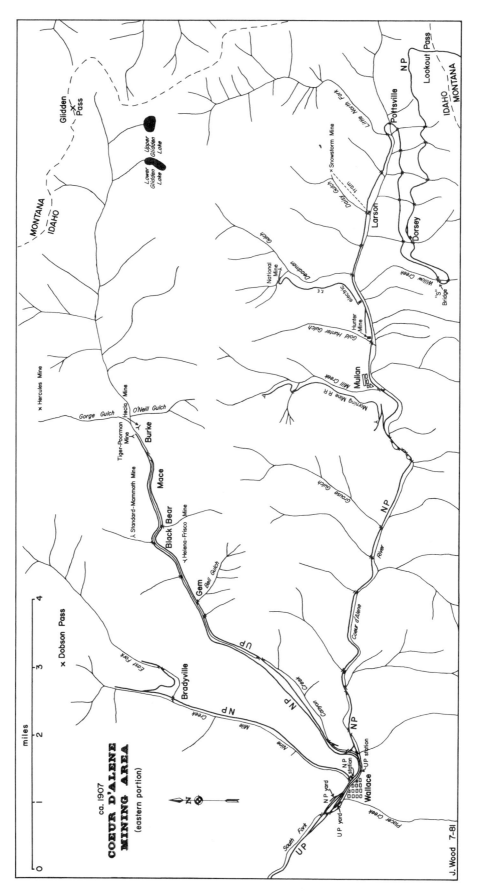

COEUR D'ALENE MINING AREA

ca. 1907

(eastern portion)

J. Wood 7-81

F. J. Haynes Foundation Collection
Montana Historical Society

Trains bound for the Coeur d'Alene Branch originated at Missoula, Montana, although the branch really diverged from the main line several miles to the west at DeSmet. When this photograph of the Missoula depot was taken by Haynes in 1894, the Coeur d'Alene Branch had been in operation about three years. This beautiful wooden building was apparently the second depot, and it in turn was soon replaced by the present brick one.

This praise of the new line was common to each new railroad built into the area, and this is no surprise as more competition brought lower rates. One example of lower rates was the cost for a passenger to travel between Wallace and Missoula. Before the Coeur d'Alene Branch was finished the trip cost $16.20 and afterward it was only $7.55.

In addition to the utilitarian aspect of opening travel to the east for passengers and freight, the new line unveiled spectacular scenery for the tourist. The NP claimed "The rugged mountain scenery is of the finest along the railroad," and the *Helena Independent* called the "grand mountain scenery" equal to that of any railroad in the United States and especially compared it to the Denver & Rio Grande line over Marshall Pass. Closer to home the *Wallace Press* proclaimed;

The ride from Lookout to Mullan is the most picturesque of the trip. At one point there are visible three tracks, one below the other, and the farthest down looks like two strands of wire. To illustrate how the road winds: at one point in a direct line it is but four miles to Mullan yet the railroad goes thirteen miles to reach it.

It didn't take long for the scenic new branch to attract the adventurous, but not all benefited the line. On November 19, 1891, a train bound for Mullan was boarded by "two visitors" above Pottsville and the express messenger R. R. Case was "relieved" of $2,800. The culprits were never found. Unfortunately this was not the only type of difficulty the line experienced.

The cost of constructing the line was extremely high. A *Wallace Press* report claimed, "The road is said to be the most expensive constructed in the Northwest, costing $65,000 per mile. An expenditure of $70,000 is being made on improvements which will make it one of the safest and best equiped in the country." But the profits were barely meet-

DE SMET & CŒUR D'ALENE BRANCH.

	Pass. Daily, Ex. Sun.	Express Daily, Ex. Sun.	Miles	STATIONS. Via Steamer from Mission to Coeur d'Alene	Express Daily.	Pass. Daily, Ex. Sun.	
Mixed trains lv. Wallace 9.20 AM: Gem 9.40 AM, ar. Burke 10.15 AM Daily, ex Sun. Leave Wallace 4.15 PM. Gem 4.35 PM, ar. Burke 5 10 PM. Daily.	....	2 15 p.m	0	Lv...Helena....Ar	10 45 p.m.	....	Mixed trains lv. Burke 11.15 AM, Gem 11.35 AM, ar. Wallace 12 05 PM Daily, ex. Sun. Lv. Burke 6.15 PM, ar. Wallace 6 45 PM Daily.
	....	8.15 a.m	125	Lv...Missoula...Ar	6.05 "	....	
	....	8.30 a.m.	131	Lv...De Smet....Ar	5 50 "	....	
	....	8 58 "	142	....Frenchtown.....	5.22 "	....	
	....	9.12 "	146	.......Huson......	5.05 "	....	
	....	9 37 "	156	....Lothrop......	4.43 "	....	
	....	10.22 "	173	.......Rivulet.....	3 58 "	....	
	....	11.05 "	189	...Iron Mountain...	3.14 "	....	
	....	11.19 "	195	...Spring Gulch....	3 00 "	....	
	....	11.48 a.m.	205	....St Regis.......	2 30 "	....	
	....	12 50 p.m.	227	.....Saltese.......	1.10 p.m.	....	
	....	2 57 "	253	......Mullan......	11.30 a.m.	....	
	12 15 p.m	3 20 p.m.	259	Ar...Wallace....Lv	11.00 a.m.	Ar 4 00 PM	
	....	....	266	Ar....Burke....Lv	....	....	
	12 35 p.m	7 25 p.m.	264	Ar....Osborn....Lv	8.40 a.m.	3.41 p.m.	
	12 55 "	8 00 "	270	...Wardner Jct..Ar	8.10 "	3 17 "	
	1 35 "	8 45 "	279	....Kingston......	7.30 "	2 45 "	
	2 00 p.m	9.15 p.m.	284	Ar....Mission....Lv	7.00 a.m	2 15 "	
	....	....	284	Lv....Mission....Ar	....	....	
	*5 55 p.m	....	334	Lv. Cœur d'Alene .Ar.	....	+8 40 a.m.	
	6.30 "	....	343	...Post Falls.....	....	8.05 "	
	6 40 "	....	350	...Hauser Jct.....	....	7.55 "	
	*7 35 p.m.	....	371	Ar....Spokane....Lv	....	7.05 a.m.	

Early Coeur d'Alene Branch timetable from the summer of 1893. Narrow gauge service as well as service between Spokane and Coeur d'Alene are shown.

Heading west the Coeur d'Alene Branch met and followed the Missoula (now Clark Fork) River downstream. This 1894 Haynes view looking east shows the considerable trestle work that was necessary along the river.

West of the previous view the Coeur d'Alene Branch passed through tunnel No. 2 on its way to the town of St. Regis (there the tracks left the Clark Fork and headed up the St. Regis de Borgia River). Here, at the east entrance of the tunnel, the superintendent's car and party pose before heading on to Wallace. The end detail of the car is quite evident, including a Miller coupler (an early replacement for the dangerous link and pin type). It was the mismatch of an OR&N Miller coupler with another type that caused the first fatal railroad accident in the Coeur d'Alenes (mentioned in Chapter Seven).

Another 1894 view of tunnel No. 2 and the Clark Fork River this time facing east. Note the large amount of earth work necessary in the construction of the line.

ing operating expenses due to the competition of the OR&N, low silver prices, and labor difficulties in the mines. Regardless of the causes, the cost of construction really alarmed President Villard in 1891 as he traveled over the line. In the span of a few years capital intended to cover construction for many years was wiped out building the Coeur d'Alene Branch and other lines in the Northwest. His alarm was justified as coming events were to soon show.

The year of 1892 began with most of the mine owners on the South Fork closing their mines ostensibly to force the railroads to lower freight rates, but apparently they were more interested in lowering miners wages. The resulting violence came to be known as the "Mining War of 1892."

In June Wallace did get a brief taste of what it would be like to have a transcontinental railroad passing through town.

In order to gain elevation climbing the east side of the Bitter Root Mountains, the Coeur d'Alene Branch makes two loops and passes through the Borax (No. 3) tunnel. This east facing Haynes photograph shows the lowest line along the St. Regis River on the far left, the middle line, and the upper line with the last car of the 1894 Superintendent's Special bound for Wallace.

Hiram H. Wilcox Photo
F. J. Haynes Foundation Collection
Montana Historical Society

A later view (1899) of the Borax tunnel taken further up the hill reveals the Borax station on the middle line complete with water tank and sand tower.

The *Coeur d'Alene Miner* of June twenty-fifth explained:

The burning of a large bridge east of Hope has caused the traffic, freight and passenger, of the main line of the Northern Pacific to come through the Coeur d'Alenes from Missoula to Spokane over the Union Pacific track. This necessitated bringing railroad men and engines having headquarters at Hope to this city, which makes Wallace today the greatest railroad town in Idaho. This town is full of railroad bells, shrieking of whistles and rumbling of cars.

Great transcontinental passenger trains, made up of two locomotives, half a dozen baggage cars, mail car, eimgrant cars, day coaches, dining car and Pullman sleepers, were a decided novelty to our citizens, who have become accustomed of late to see nothing but a string of boxcars with a passenger coach bringing up the rear, and when the first great passenger train arrived last Sunday the rain did not prevent a large number from assembling at the depot.

A number of heavy engines (hogs) in addition to the one stationed here help pull the trains between this city and Saltese.

The unavoidable difficulties in getting through this city frequently compels trains to lay over here several hours, which gives the pas-

F. J. Haynes Foundation Collection
Montana Historical Society

Now west of Lookout Pass and dropping toward Wallace, the 1894 Superintendent's Special pauses on the "S" bridge. The locomotive with its pilot mounted snowplow is unidentified, but it may have been one of the few 4-4-0s that ran on the branch in the early years.

Beautiful view of NP No. 478 on the Wallace turntable ca. 1890s. Note the unusual clerestory on the cab.

NP No. 76 at Wallace near the turn of the century. The pilot still carries the old link-and-pin coupler. This Class F-1 Consolidation (2-8-0) was one of many of its type used on the Coeur d'Alene Branch.

NP No. 398 on the Dorsey Trestle ca. 1902 was one of the many Ten Wheeler (4-6-0) engines used in passenger service on the Coeur d'Alene Branch. The forest behind the trestle had been recently burned by one of the many forest fires that ravaged the area.

Barnard-Stockbridge Collection
University of Idaho Library

The "new" NP depot in Wallace was completed on May 20, 1902, not long before this photograph was taken. The freight house on the left was the old station built by the CR&N that had been moved to this new location.

Standow Photo
Coeur d'Alene District Mining Museum

The interior of the NP depot is shown in this 1910 view. The numbers identify the following: 1. Rolla Breed; 2. E. E. Case; 3. Louis Oma; 4. G. Gunsenburger; 5. Fred Levering.

Barnard-Stockbridge Collection
University of Idaho Library

President Theodore Roosevelt at the Wallace depot on May 26, 1903. The President made this visit in defference to the late Senator Heyburn of Idaho, whom he admired. As had happened at previous important events, bad weather dampened the celebration. Heavy rain the night before damaged decorations and turned the unpaved streets to mud. The main decorations were $5,000 worth of American flags.

Barnard-Stockbridge Collection
University of Idaho Library

The 600-ton Hercules Concentrator below the NP freight yards at Wallace in 1910. (This was the end of NP standard gauge track.) The concentrator served the ore from the Hercules Mine above Burke. The ore was hauled down Canyon Creek by rail to this mill. Although the mine closed August 24, 1925, the mill continued to operate spradically until 1942. The last of the buildings finally burned in 1976. Levi "Al" Hutton, the CR&N-NP engineer, made his fortune as a partner in the Hercules.

Don Roberts Collection
Oregon Historical Society

The Burke local passenger train was handled by NP No. 93 in this 1909 view taken in Wallace. (The top of the depot appears above the cab.) The man second from the right is Joe Ramey and the conductor, second from the left, is Steve Eddins. The engine was a 2-8-0 that had been owned by the Montana Union (a line absorbed by the NP). It was necessary to use rather heavy engines on this run as the grade was three percent and the passenger cars were quite heavy.

R. V. Nixon Collection

NP No. 60 (another Class F-1 engine) at Wallace about 1902. The coupler on the pilot has a slot in the knuckle so it can mate with the older link-and-pin type.

C. R. Iles Photo
R. V. Nixon Collection

This view of No. 93 was taken in Wallace about 1916. It was a Class F-4 engine built by Grant in 1887.

sengers an opportunity to look over the town. Many of them express much surprise at the substantial appearance of our little city.

While the extra traffic from the main line was only temporary, the normal conditions of the line also appeared good in this detailed description of the facilities at Wallace which appeared in the *Coeur d'Alene Miner* on February 25, 1893:

The Northern Pacific has side tracks sufficient to accommodate 75 standard gauge and fifty of its narrow gauge cars, the latter operating between Wallace and Mission and making a connection with their boats on Coeur d'Alene Lake. Their accommodations for engines are two stalls on the standard gauge, while a long shed is used on the narrow gauge. Four standard gauge and two narrow gauge engines are kept here. Besides the engineers and firemen on these engines twelve men, wipers, car cleaners, hostlers, etc. find steady employment at the yard. The rotary snowplow, which has been almost a daily necessity this winter, makes this its headquarters with its crew of men.

The daily service consists of one passenger and one freight train daily on the narrow gauge, two mixed trains on the Burke Branch, and a passenger and a freight on the Missoula cutoff. The trains on the cutoff are a double-header, so that there are seven train crews running in and out of Wallace daily. Those of the narrow gauge make Wallace their home, and many of the others contribute regularly to its prosperity.

At the depot are Superintendent J. G. Boyd, Agent J. C. Mann, an assistant, an operator and a warehouse man. Then there are four section crews here, aggregating twenty men, the pay roll for whole amounting to not less than $3,000 monthly.

This prosperity didn't last long, for by the summer of 1893 the great panic affecting the whole nation forced the NP to cut passenger service on the Coeur d'Alene Branch. Now just one coach was attached to the freight trains, and they were cut to only three a week!

Finally on August fifteenth Villard's fears were realized as the NP was forced into receivership. Like the UP one of the big factors in the collapse was the high cost of construction into the mining

An eastbound NP passenger train approaches the Wallace OWR&N (UP) station on April 19, 1926. A load of express shipments is waiting by the track to be picked up.

R. V. Nixon Collection

Ten-wheeler No. 274 prepares to take the Missoula bound local out of Wallace in 1913.

Barnard-Stockbridge Collection
University of Idaho Library

The Morning Concentrator, just below Mullan, was the first major industry east of Wallace on the NP line. The Morning operated its own narrow gauge railroad between the concentrator and the mine. (This railroad is covered in Chapter Five.) The middle track in this photograph is "dual gauge" to allow the mine's narrow gauge Shays to operate in this yard.

Barnard-Stockbridge Collection
University of Idaho Library

The NP and OR&N depots at Mullan appear in this 1905 photograph. The tracks following the South Fork up from Wallace enter the picture in the upper left and pass the NP depot. In the lower right is the old OR&N depot with its tracks that were abandoned in 1894.

area and the poor return on the investment.

Following this the Coeur d'Alene Branch saw only minor changes for many years. Improvements in the facilities at Wallace were the first to be made.

Barnard-Stockbridge Collection
University of Idaho Library

This view of Mullan looking east was taken in the early 1890s. On the right the NP depot can be seen, and to the left-center the top of the OR&N depot appears. The tracks of both railroads continue up to the Hunter Concentrator in the distance. From there the NP track had been constructed over Lookout Pass. Lookout is not visible, but would be over the mountains in about the center. The low notch to the left is Mullan Pass. (Although it appears to be low it is actually over 500 feet higher than Lookout.)

The Hunter Concentrator was located a short distance above Mullan. This shows its appearance in 1910. While it had once been served by the NP and OR&N, the OR&N track had now been long abandoned.

The 500-ton National Concentrator was further up the line from the Hunter. This picture, taken in 1915, shows the long shed built on the hillside to cover an electric railroad which connected the mill to the mine. The National Mine was primarily a copper producer, but the grade of its ore was much lower than that of the Snowstorm Mine, a little further up the line. Due to the low grade ore the National didn't operate many years.

Earlier in 1891 the standard gauge facilities described in the *Coeur d'Alene Miner* were constructed. These had included a two-stall engine house and a fifty-six-foot turntable. In 1900 a new six-stall roundhouse and turntable replaced these. This new building was to serve the railroad until it was torn down in 1957. The other big change was the addition of a badly needed new depot.

If any one thing could be picked as a symbol of railroading in the Coeur d'Alenes it would be the beautiful NP depot in Wallace which stands to this day. Construction was begun in 1901 with concrete and brick on the north bank of the South Fork along Sixth Street.

The buff colored bricks used in construction reportedly came from the huge Hotel Olympic in Tacoma. (This was a project of the NP that the 1893 panic aborted.) The bricks had been made in China and were imported by the NP in

This four-car NP passenger train battles across the "S" bridge on its way to Lookout Pass. The engine is a 4-6-0, apparently No. 365. This spectacular shot was copied from a very faded postcard.

1890 — perhaps as ballast in ships holds. The Wallace depot used 15,000 of them and the Missoula depot 58,255. The concrete portion was made from cement and tailings from the concentrators in the area.

The original CR&N depot which had been located just to the south was moved to the north end of the new depot and there served as a freight house until razed in 1974.

When completed on May 20, 1902, a total of $9,368.21 had been spent. It was described in the *Illustrated History of North Idaho* as "an elegant brick and

NP No. 1223 (a 2-8-0) handling an eastbound extra on the Coeur d'Alene Branch July 10, 1910. (This was about one month before the great 1910 forest fire.) The location appears to be the siding just above Dorsey.

The large trestle at Dorsey, shown here in the 1890s, was a few miles above the "S" bridge. To reach here trains left Mullan (out of the picture to the left) and headed up the South Fork (not visible along the bottom of the canyon). At Pottsville (over the ridge in the center) the track looped back to the left. This is the lower line that is visible. It climbed to the left where another loop was made at the "S" bridge. Continuing up the grade brought trains to Dorsey. (The station is at the far side of the trestle.) Just beyond the station and "cut" was a short siding and a water tank. After the siding there was about three more miles of four percent grade before Lookout Pass was reached. The station at Dorsey was a popular picture taking site, and a number of examples of these appear elsewhere in this book.

Barnard-Stockbridge Collection
University of Idaho Library

This eastbound mixed train at Lookout Pass is probably an example of the cutback in passenger service after the 1893 Panic. The recently erected sign reads, "Coeur d'Alene Divide — Idaho : Montana — Elevation 4,680 Ft. Above Sea Level."

Montana Historical Society

The town of Taft, Montana was nine miles below Lookout to the east. The NP station was the small building in the center with the order board sticking out to the right. The track to the right leads to Lookout. Although the town was literally right on the NP track (it passed down the main street), it was the Chicago, Milwaukee & St. Paul Railroad that gave the town its prosperity during this time (1907–1908). Many of these men were working on the Milwaukee's 9,000 foot St. Paul tunnel which was a short distance away.

Montana Historical Society

Saltese, Montana (5 miles east of Taft) was the NP terminal for helper engines boosting trains up the four percent grade to Lookout (toward the right). A two-stall engine house and a turntable are at the lower left. Up the track to the right is the two-story depot. (This building was similar to many other NP depots — including ones at Iron Mountain and Mullan.) A little further to the right is the water tank. At the time this photograph was taken in 1908 the Milwaukee was constructing its line above the town. Work had just begun on the huge trestle which would run parallel to the NP track.

Bill Pike Collection
Courtesy Mineral County Historical Book 1976

The rear of the Saltese NP depot is shown here with the 1910 baseball team from De Borgia (a station stop nine miles to the east).

R. V. Nixon Collection

NP No. 3005, a Class Z 2-6-6-2, was one of the first articulated engines used on the Coeur d'Alene Branch. They were able to replace double-headed Consolidations on many freights. The Class Z engines, numbered 3000-3015, were built by Baldwin in 1907. This ca. 1910 photograph was probably taken at Saltese, which was near the start of the four percent grade over Lookout Pass.

R. V. Nixon Collection

NP No. 3100 was a Class Z-1 Mallet, the second type of articulated used on the Coeur d'Alene Branch. This view was taken at Saltese in 1911. The No. 3100 was sold to Polson Logging Company in 1940, and later went to Rayonnier.

Montana Historical Society

St. Regis, Montana, is about 24 miles east of Saltese. The NP depot is on the right. This photograph was taken ca. 1909 after construction of the line to Paradise, Montana (the lower track). The track to Wallace curves off left behind the depot. After the terrible flooding in the spring of 1933 the NP abandoned its damaged track between here and Haugan (18.7 miles to the west). An agreement was made to use the Milwaukee track over this distance.

concrete edifice, ornate and picturesque . . ." and the truth of these words can still be seen today.

Now however, after serving over 78 years, the BN closed the depot on September 3, 1980, along with its abandonment of the whole Coeur d'Alene Branch. While the building is now included on the National Register of Historic Places, its future is far from being certain. Hopefully it can be maintained as a valuable part of the historic heritage of the area.

Outside the town of Wallace the biggest change in the Coeur d'Alene Branch was the construction of a 21.8-mile line between St. Regis, Mon-

Bill Pike Collection
Courtesy Mineral County Historical Book 1976

This icy water tank and coal dock were at Rivulet, Montana, which was 30 miles east of St. Regis on the NP. The time was winter in 1920.

R. V. Nixon Collection

NP No. 401 (a 2-6-0) at Rivulet about 1916. This type of locomotive was quite light and seldom used on the Coeur d'Alene Branch.

Marvin Jones Collection

The Fish Creek trestle east of Rivulet was one of the tallest trestles on the Montana portion of the Coeur d'Alene Branch. This photograph (taken from a color postcard) was made prior to 1915 when a new all steel viaduct replaced this largely wood structure.

McKay Photo
W. R. McGee Collection

The Wallace bound passenger train (on right) makes connections with the double-headed NP No. 1 North Coast Limited at Missoula in 1903. The light Wallace train is headed by 4-4-0 No. 753 while the Limited has helper No. 1212 (a 2-8-0) and Pacific No. 2413 (4-6-2). Note the unusual compound cylinders on No. 1212.

John Fahey Collection

The *Georgie Oakes* at the Old Mission landing. The *Georgie Oakes* was built by the NP in 1891 to replace the ore-hauler *Coeur d'Alene*. The cabins from the *Coeur d'Alene* were used on the *Georgie Oakes*, and the old hull became a barge (shown in this photograph). In the lower right is a flatcar of the CR&N narrow gauge loading freight.

tana, on the branch and Paradise, Montana, on the NP main line. The purpose of this new construction was to provide a "water level" grade for freight trains and thus eliminate the heavy grades over Evaro Hill, which was west of Missoula. Since the new line would be 28 miles longer, faster trains would still use the original main line.

Construction which included improvements in the line between DeSmet and St. Regis was started at the end of 1906, and operation was begun on February 6, 1909. This reduced the true Coeur d'Alene Branch to the line between Wallace and St. Regis.

Another very interesting development in the story of the branch surfaced at the end of 1908. The original plan to tunnel through the Bitter Root Mountains was revived. The opportunity arose as the Chicago, Milwaukee & St. Paul finished their 9,000-foot tunnel at St. Paul Pass. Their facilities for constructing the eastern end of their tunnel were located at Taft, Montana. Taft was also on the Coeur d'Alene Branch and very near Lookout Pass. The *Railway Age Gazette* reported the plan on December 11, 1908:

This company [NP] bought from the CM&StP the power plant near Taft, Montana, preliminary to commencing work on a two-mile tunnel in the neighborhood of Lookout Mountain, Montana. The western end of the tunnel will be near Dorsey, Idaho, and the eastern end near the St. Regis river. These improvements are to be made to straighten and shorten the present NP line.

But for some unknown reason the tunneling project was again dropped. However, it is certain that the great forest fire of 1910 destroyed the power plant, and if the tunnel was still under consideration at that time this destruction probably doomed the project.

Thus trains on the Coeur d'Alene Branch were destined to battle up the

T. W. Marsh Photo
Robert Pearson Collection

Both the OR&N and NP facilities below Wallace appear in this view taken in the late 1890s. Decrepit equipment of the CR&N sits on the track in the foreground — boxcar No. 6, a flatcar, a caboose (made from a boxcar), and a lonely coach at the end. Narrow gauge track still extends down the canyon just to the right of center. The narrow gauge also connects with the dual gauge turntable. The track above the turntable is NP standard gauge. The rear of a rotary snowplow and its tender can be seen just beyond the turntable. Behind its tender (where the smoke is rising) is the front of a "cap-stacked" Consolidation heading a freight train. The nearest water tank is NP, but the one to its right in the distance is OR&N. Also in the distance to the left of the NP tank the large OR&N coaling bunker is visible.

Barnard-Stockbridge Collection
University of Idaho Library

The Wallace depot of the CR&N (here owned by the NP) after the Coeur d'Alene Branch from Missoula reached town. The standard gauge track nearest the camera belonged to the OR&N. The next track (belonging to the NP) is dual gauge, which allowed both the NP standard gauge and CR&N narrow gauge trains the use of the station. The cause of the celebration, with the band playing to the right of the station, has been lost, but it is possible that it could be one of the first excursions over the Coeur d'Alene Branch in the summer of 1891.

four percent grade on one side of the divide only to fight to keep the train from running away coming down an equally steep grade on the other side, a situation that would last as long as the line.

The Narrow Gauge

When the NP began operating the CR&N in the fall of 1888 they found the condition of the line had been allowed to deteriorate by the previous owners in their effort to squeeze a maximum profit before the transfer of the line. Within a year of the take over the NP had to spend $21,400 in badly needed track repairs between the Mission and Wallace. The operating equipment was also a great problem.

Not only were there not enough cars, but those that existed were in bad condition. The master mechanic, T. A. Helm, and six other men were often busy day and night keeping the narrow gauge rolling stock in order. And when the line needed a different type of car they modified what they had.

For several years there were no cabooses on the line and regular boxcars were used in their place. Even more surprising, the same boxcars were used to carry passengers on mixed trains (passenger and freight)! Finally the shop converted two of the boxcars into "regular" cabooses by adding windows, end doors, and end platforms. In the winter of 1889 another of the boxcars was also converted for postal-express service.

The machine shops where this work was conducted had been moved from the Mission to Wallace in the winter of 1888. (Here the word "moved" should be taken literally as some buildings were actually carried up the line on flat cars.) These "new" facilities for the narrow gauge were located below Wallace. The original narrow gauge engine shed

east of town was pulled down by the end of the year. The new machine shop was 16 x 56 feet and a temporary engine shed 16 x 150 feet. The engine shed, which could hold four engines, was to be replaced by a large roundhouse the next spring, but this never happened. Also to be completed were a coach house and a water tank.

The truly primitive conditions of the railroad were reflected by a description of the depot in Wallace. When a beautiful new regulator clock with a cherry case was added in December of 1888, the remark was made that it would be nice to have the correct time for a change; however, since the trains seldom ran on time this made little difference. This created a real problem for ladies that had to wait when the trains didn't leave at the advertised time, for there were no chairs or seats! The men had already learned not to go to the depot until they heard the whistle blow.

The depot also lacked a telegraph or telephone. Operation on the line required that trains scheduled into a station needed to clear that station before another train could leave in the opposite direction. If a train broke down a runner would need to be sent ahead to report to the next station before another train could move. By the end of 1888 Wallace did have one telephone in the Wallace Hotel which improved the situation somewhat.

These were the conditions on January 26, 1889, when the *Wallace Free Press* reported the following humorous predicament:

Last Thursday morning the freight which usually arrives early in the morning from Mission, was very late. The passenger train went to Burke and returned, did the usual amount of switching and was ready to go below. As no word had been received from the freight it was expected to arrive at any moment, and the pas-

The gleaming "Big Four" being wooded up somewhere along the line soon after its delivery. The man in the cab is possibly Mac Mortimer, the first engineer to serve on the engine. The photograph was in a series titled "Views on the Northern Pacific RR."

senger train was waiting for it. Some time after the usual time for the train to leave some one at Wardner Junction called the telephone operator here [in the Wallace Hotel] and asked if the passenger train had left here. The response was prompt that it had. Nothing more was thought of the matter until about noon, when the telephone operator was agained [sic] summoned. It was Wardner Junction again and the party wanted Conductor Ed Babb. The operator responded that Mr. Babb left here several hours ago with his regular train. This didn't go, however, for Babb happened to be standing in hearing distance and interruped the conversation. He went to the telephone and answered the call. The gentleman at the other end was Conductor Ed Brown on the freight train, who was side tracked at the Junction like Babb was here, each waiting for the other to pass.

It is no wonder that a list of needs for Wallace carried in this issue of the newspaper included "another railroad!" and a "telegraph line!"

Not withstanding the primitiveness of the line, the depot in Wallace saw $13,000 in total receipts in November of 1888 which reflected about 2,000 tons or over 150 carloads of ore. By May of the following year the NP auditor reported the CR&N had net earnings of $92,569 to be divided among the stockholders.

One of the biggest improvements the NP made in the narrow gauge was the addition of a new locomotive. The first three locomotives were so light that each could only pull seven cars over the

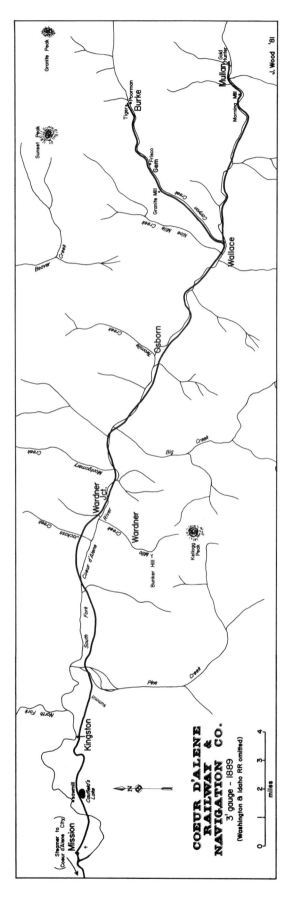

hills at Kingston and Pine Creek, and this number only in very good weather. Therefore, before the end of 1888, the NP placed an order with the Baldwin Locomotive Works for a 37-ton engine which was expected to easily handle ten cars over the same grades. While this engine would give the advantage of longer trains, its weight would also necessitate strengthening all the track and bridges.

With the arrival of spring in 1889 crews were put to work laying heavier rails and strengthening bridges with extra stringers. But when the "monster locomotive" arrived on April twenty-third the only heavy rail finished was between Wallace and Mullan. Thus No. 4's trial run on May sixth was to Mullan with T. A. Helm at the throttle. Mac Mortimer was scheduled as the regular engineer of the "Big Four" (as she came to be known), and together they were soon handling freight runs.

The addition of this new engine allowed time for much needed repairs of the "pioneer locomotives," No. 1 and No. 2. In April of 1890 the *Wallace Free Press* described the rebuilding:

Last Monday T. A. Helm, Master Mechanic of the Coeur d'Alene Railway and Navigation Company's shops here, turned out what may be considered a new engine. The oldest machine on the road, no. 1, broken down and dilapidated, was put into his hands several months ago. It was worn out, and needed so much repairing that the company was ready to cast it aside as worthless. Mr. Helm, however, took the decrepit steed in charge, and gave it such a grooming that it now looks as if it had just come out of the big Baldwin works at Philadelphia. A trial run was made with it down to the Mission and back on Monday, Mr. Helm getting into the cab and handling the reins. The trip was made without a jar or hitch, and every piece of the little horse worked like a charm.

Two months later no. 2 was likewise turned out in "new condition."

Earlier in the spring of 1889 the

three-foot gauge rails had reached the Hunter concentrator above Mullan (as related earlier in this chapter) and the narrow gauge had reached its greatest extent — slightly over thirty-nine miles including the branch to Burke. The narrow gauge continued to do good business with the receipts at the Wallace depot of $9,000 in August and $15,000 in September. Even when the OR&N reached Wallace that winter F. W. Gilbert, superintendent of the CR&N, declared their business remained the same. However, their freight rates were drastically cut as much as seven dollars per ton in January, which reflected the damage already done by the OR&N competition.

While the OR&N brought lower rates and better service to the area, the people still had a tender spot in their hearts for the CR&N and its employees. Two of the most popular employees were conductor Ed Babb and engineer Levi "Al" Hutton. One of several interesting stories involving Al Hutton appeared in the *Wallace Free Press* on March 16, 1889. It is certain that this story must have resulted in a good teasing of Hutton.

The Ghost of Swingdoor Cabin

The Swingdoor Cabin, named for its door hung from above by leather straps, was a refuge built during work on the Mullan Road. It was located 1½ miles west of Wallace on the line of the Coeur d'Alene Ry. & Nav. Co. During the past few months the freight train has been leaving here at about 7 o'clock for Mission, and as is well known, Al Hutton is the engineer and Horace Smith fireman. On the night of which we write the train pulled out about two hours late. The train passed Swingdoor Cabin between 9 & 10 o'clock and the snow was falling quite rapidly. They were making a curve around the cabin when a figure appeared a few rods ahead of them on the track, the sight of which made Hutton's hair stand and Smith's teeth chatter. It was a female figure, dressed in a long white robe, her hair falling loosely over her shoulders, and she tripped noiselessly along at a speed equal to that of the train. Presently the mysterious figure vanished and Hutton and Smith breathed once more. It had been seen once or twice since then, but the engineer and fireman are not looking for ghosts any more.

But not all of the CR&N employees were as popular as Hutton and Babb. Efforts of superintendent Gilbert to economize the line brought him local condemnation. Blaming Gilbert for the poor condition of the road, the *Wallace Free Press* in November of 1889 ran an article titled "A Very Narrow-Gauge

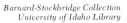

Barnard-Stockbridge Collection
University of Idaho Library
This blast next to the Wallace depot was an attempt to clear the channel of the South Fork during a high spring run-off (a frequent problem). Just beyond the depot is a CR&N narrow gauge boxcar and an NP standard gauge caboose. Also note the interesting birdhouse on the right in the photograph.

Road" in which it was claimed "His sole purpose is to economize and stint the service." Gilbert was also accused of overworking employees which were praised for still being zealous in behalf of the company. Therefore great approval followed the next year when he was promoted and transferred to the Idaho Division and Robert R. Colwell (popular local agent of the CR&N) was moved to the job of superintendent.

It was also about this time that some unnamed individual first dubbed the CR&N the "Chippy Line." (This was in reference to the houses of ill repute on the line.) While this nickname received widespread usage, this same person's name for the OR&N, the "Jumbo," was quickly forgotten. Perhaps this was due to the affection the public had for the former.

Although only four years old, the CR&N narrow gauge was running out of time. The standard gauge OR&N was now a reality and construction of the Coeur d'Alene Branch from Missoula called for spreading the narrow gauge rails between the Hunter concentrator and Wallace. The work was reported in the *Wallace Press* July 25, 1891.

No more narrow-gauge trains will run to Mullan. The last toot of a "chippy" engine was heard at the east end on Thursday [July 23] morning. Immediately afterward a force of men under Civil Engineer Cantine commenced the work of widening the track from the Hunter mill, and by evening, a broad-gauge engine could have run down to the Morning mill. As fast as the rails are widened out a construction train comes along to surface the roadbed. It will take till Sunday afternoon to reach Wallace. A very substantial roadbed is being made along the whole line.

This task was soon completed and by the end of the year the branch to Burke was also standard gauged.

Now reduced to about 24 miles, the narrow gauge entered her declining

Barnard-Stockbridge Collection
University of Idaho Library

Wallace after the 1890 fire which destroyed the town. The CR&N depot (roof showing in the foreground) was not touched. To the left of the depot is a very rare shot of the "Big Four" on the line. Just beyond the engine next to the river is the standard gauge track of the OR&N.

DE SMET, CŒUR D'ALENE, AND HAUSER BRANCHES.

Daily mixed train leaves Wallace 4 45 p. m., arrives Burke 5 45 p. m., also another leaves Wallace 8 15 a. m., arrives Burke 9 15 a. m., except Sunday.	Mixed. Daily Ex. Sun.	Mixed. Daily Ex. Sun.	Miles.	STATIONS. Via Steamer from Mission to Cœur d'Alene.	Mixed. Daily Ex. Sun.	Mixed. Daily Ex. Sun.	Daily mixed train leaves Burke 6 35 p. m., arrives Wallace 7 35 p. m., also another leaves Burke, daily except Sunday, 10 00 a.m., arrives Wallace 11 00 a. m.
		7 30 AM	0	Lv. **Helena** Ar	5 15 PM		
		7 55 "	125	Lv. **Missoula** Ar	4 50 "		
		8 30 "	131	....De Smet..Ar	4 10 "		
		*8 50 "	142	...Frenchtown..	*3 50 "		
		*10 43 "	146	.....Huson....	* 1 55		
		11 50 "	173	....Rivulet....	12 20 PM		
		*12 40 PM	189	.Iron Mountain.	*11 59 AM		
		* 1 15 "	195	.Spring Gulch..	*11 50 "		
		2 30 "	205	...St. Regis...	9 55 "		
		4 35 "	227	....Saltese....	7 45 "		
	11 25 AM	5 15 "	253	...**Mullan**...	7 15 AM	4 00 PM	
			259	Ar. **Wallace** Lv			
			266	Ar...**Burke**..Lv			
	11 45 AM		261	Ar..Osborne..Lv		3 35 PM	
	12 15 PM		270	..**Wardner**.Ar		3 05 "	
	12 55 "		279	...Kingston...		2 20 "	
	1 15 PM		284	...Mission..Lv		1 55 "	
			284	Lv...Mission...Ar			
	8 30 AM		334	Lv **Cr d'Alene** Ar		6 00 PM	
	9 05 "		343	...**Post Falls**..		5 25 "	
	9 15 "		350	..Hauser Jct..		5 15 "	
	10 05 AM		371	Ar. **Spokane**. Lv		4 30 PM	

This November 29, 1896, timetable was probably the last to list service on the narrow gauge. From this time on passengers traveling west from Wallace had to use the OR&N.

years which were nevertheless punctuated by occasional bright spots. In the winter of 1891 the great Bunker Hill, which normally shipped ore by the OR&N, switched to the narrow gauge. The ore was carried to Wallace and then transferred to the NP standard gauge for the trip east. While this was an expensive operation, it provided a method to pressure the OR&N which had previously had a virtual monopoly on shipping Bunker Hill ore. Soon an agreement was made with the OR&N for them to turn over ore from the mines in

the Wardner area which wished to ship by the NP. This was done at either Wallace or Spokane, and in return the NP provided a similar service in areas the UP track didn't reach.

As mentioned earlier the year of 1892 was the start of hard times in the area. The NP, seeing the "writing on the wall," sold the "Big Four" in December to the East Broad Top Railroad & Coal Company of Rockhill Furnace, Pennsylvania. (Apparently the most valuable locomotive was sold first to salvage as much as possible from their investment.) A couple of months later in February of 1893 No. 3 was sold for $2,076 to a James Richardson in Philadelphia. This left only the two "pioneer engines" which had been overhauled by T. A. Helm to finish out the declining years of the narrow gauge.

Hard times continued for the great panic of 1893 affected the whole nation. In the mining area the OR&N was forced to cut out all passenger service, and that sent some business to the narrow gauge. The narrow gauge also carried a considerable amount of cordwood from Kingston for the mines in

Bert Ward Collection

This coach may have belonged to the CR&N. It was acquired by the White Pass and Yukon and the original owner was forgotten. However, it was discovered that the original trucks under No. 216 and another coach No. 214 had been overstamped by the NP. Since the CR&N was the only narrow gauge operated by the NP, it is likely that these two cars were part of the CR&N equipment reportedly sold in Alaska during 1898.

Burke, with the Poorman alone accounting for a use of twenty-four cords a day.

But regardless of this spurt of business the CR&N, like the giant NP, fell into receivership during the year. On October 10, 1893, Henry Stanton and John Huntoon were appointed receivers. They allowed the NP to continue operating the line.

In the summer of 1894 a fire in the engine shed damaged both remaining narrow gauge locomotives. They were shipped east for repairs (probably to Missoula) and a temporary replacement was sought. While this was not found, one of the damaged engines (it is not clear which one) was returned on September first and put into service. Before the end of the month, as luck would have it, this same locomotive collided with a boxcar four miles below Wardner and had to be shipped back to Missoula for more repairs!

At the time this last accident took place the narrow gauge was "rushed with business," and now they were again without a locomotive. From this point the final days of the narrow gauge are rather obscure. As late as 1896 the narrow gauge appeared on the NP timetable, and since the *Georgie Oakes* was pulled off the run to Mission at the end of the year, it is probable that this was the end of operation. Nevertheless the CR&N was purchased by the NP for $220,000 on January 26, 1897, the main reason being to acquire the portions already standard gauged.

The rails between the Mission and Wardner were finally torn up in March of 1898. At this time there was still talk of standard gauging the track between Wallace and Wardner to provide access to the Bunker Hill and Sullivan ore, in case there was trouble with the OR&N in hauling the NP ore over its tracks in the future.

The remaining engines, No. 1 and No. 2 were also apparently sold in 1898, or possibly in 1899, to a used equipment dealer in Chicago. It also appears that the two passenger coaches were sold to the White Pass & Yukon Railway in 1898, and other equipment may have gone there as well.

The last section of track from Wallace to Wardner was not removed until 1902, thus closing the epilogue on the story of the gallant little narrow gauge that opened the Coeur d'Alenes to the world.

Chapter Five

The Field Broadens

WITH THE ARRIVAL OF RAILROADS IN the Coeur d'Alenes came many schemes to extend the rails up side canyons to serve remote mines. The mine owners knew that a lack of rail transportation often made the difference between fortune or failure. Although many branch lines were planned, few were ever built, and even fewer were successful. The first route for a branch line and the most successful, was up Canyon Creek Canyon (first spelled Cañon Creek). This creek joins the South Fork from the north at the eastern end of Wallace.

The Canyon Creek Branches

Among the earliest claims in the South Fork country was that of the Tiger Mine on Canyon Creek. The year following its discovery in 1884 it was sold to S. S. Glidden for $35,000. Glidden soon had 3,000 tons of ore ready to be shipped, but no economical method was available. It is no wonder that Glidden became one of the foremost promoters of railroad construction into the Coeur d'Alenes. The construction of the CR&N by D. C. Corbin was in part due to Glidden's encouragement.

When construction of the CR&N didn't move fast enough Glidden incorporated the Canyon Creek Railroad on July 6, 1887, to build a three-foot gauge line from his Tiger Mine (at the future site of Burke) to Wallace. The incorporators were S. S. Glidden, Harry M.

Glidden, Frank R. Culbertson, Alexander H. Tarbet, and Charles W. O'Neil.

Little work had been done when (on September 5, 1887) Glidden signed a contract to finish the roadbed and sell the line to Corbin. Now actual construction was rapidly pushed in an attempt to cover the distance of seven miles before the winter would force a halt. The mines in the canyon were counting heavily on the railroad, and it was estimated that 100,000 tons of ore were piled awaiting shipment.

Nevertheless, construction progressed slowly with only three miles of track laid by mid-November. The rails and fish plates used on this construction were secondhand from the Utah and Northern (a narrow gauge line in the process of being standard gauge). The first shipment of ore by rail from the Wallace area was made December 12, 1887, with one carload from the Granite Mill on the lower part of Canyon Creek.

The narrow gauge track finally reached Burke (then called Bayard) where a celebration was held on December twenty-second. The train arrived about 4 P.M. greeted by the Murray brass band. S. S. Glidden gave a speech and then drove a silver spike commemorating the completion of the line.

Now that the railroad had reached Burke the area really began to boom. Although the first ore shipped from Burke

This early view of the Granite Mill near the mouth of Canyon Creek shows three flatcars of the CR&N narrow gauge. The Granite Mine was really in the canyon of Nine Mile Creek across the ridge in the background. The two were connected with an aerial tram.

Burke, Idaho — 1888. By this date the narrow gauge CR&N track had been laid through the center of town, the Tiger Mill finished on the left, and the Poorman Mill was under construction on the right.

(December thirty-first) consisted of only two carloads from the Poorman Mill, within a year there were not enough cars to handle all the Canyon Creek ore. The Tiger could ship six cars a day and the Poorman 120 tons a day or about ten carloads. And by 1889 a day came when 18 carloads were shipped from the Tiger-Poorman with the narrow gauge making about $1000 from the transaction.

While it appeared that civilization had reached Burke, the conditions on the narrow gauge were still very primitive. Operation was very casual on this branch as it was on the rest of the line. During the first year the branch operated (1887), it was reported that all trains made a fifteen minute stop at J. H. Johnson's saloon at Gem on their seven-mile trip between Wallace and Burke. Perhaps the passengers were driven to drink by their deluxe passenger accommodations, a boxcar!

The use of boxcars to carry passengers was not just a matter of economizing. The three percent grade and short curves made it impossible for the narrow gauge locomotives to haul a heavy passenger car up the grade. A slight improvement was made for passengers in the spring of 1888 when two boxcars were converted to cabooses and placed in mixed service to Burke, but this "improvement" did not satisfy the passengers for long. In 1889 the newspaper aired complaints about the "rickety box" that the women should not have to put up with. It was suggested that the railroad could at least pay to have it painted and remodeled.

But now that the NP operated the line (starting October 1, 1888), these complaints eventually produced results which were reported by the *Wallace Free Press* of October 26, 1889.

The Canyon Creek railroad is almost being converted into a new road. The twists and turns, more appropriately styled "kinks" are being taken out and in a few weeks the "Virginia worm fence" will be a little more respectable as a railroad.

When the work is completed a passenger coach is going to be put in from Wallace to Burke. . . .

Perhaps the real reason for these improvements was not the complaints, but the rapid approach of the OR&N line which reached Wallace on December 9, 1889. The concern of the NP was justified, for with the coming of spring the OR&N began surveying and grading up Canyon Creek. The NP now saw it could not keep its competition out, so it negotiated an agreement with the UP over its construction to Burke in an attempt to keep some control of the situation. This agreement was signed on June 4, 1890.

Now the OR&N really pushed its grading and soon claimed to have 500 men at work in the canyon. By the end of September tracklaying had begun, and on November 18, 1890, the OR&N was completed through the center of Burke to the Tiger and Poorman mills. This occasioned a friendly exchange between the CR&N (NP) narrow gauge and the OR&N (UP) standard gauge: "On Tuesday 'Big Four' of the Northern Pacific and the monster construction engine of the UP stood side by side between the Tiger and Poorman concentrators and the engineer shook hands out of their cabs." (*Wallace Miner*, November 22, 1890.)

The close proximity of these tracks gives some idea of the problem involved in crowding a stream, a town, and two railroads at the bottom of a narrow canyon hardly wide enough to carry the stream alone! In later years this congestion at the bottom of the canyon

Looking down canyon from the upper end of Burke. The small building with the word "Burke" superimposed on it was the CR&N depot. A sign protruding from the left side of the building proclaimed "tickets." To the right of the depot is the "Glidden House." This was a boardinghouse for the Tiger employees and later was called the Tiger Hotel. This original building burned soon after this and was rebuilt further up the canyon. On the left is the Poorman Mill.

The OR&N Burke depot which was built in the winter of 1890. This scene is complete with a cute dog as mascot.

Lower Burke in 1907. The Hecla Mine on the right and the Tiger-Poorman in the distance. Tracing the NP track on the left you come to the two-story NP depot. The OR&N depot and its track are above and to the right of the NP depot.

prompted *Ripley's Believe It Or Not* to refer to it. The story went that approaching trains blew their whistles as a signal for owners to move their cars from the roadway which ran up the track and for store owners to raise awnings to allow the trains to pass. Actually it appears that the trains would clear the awnings, but the owners would raise them to prevent hot cinders from burning them.

Notwithstanding this lack of room the second line was completed, and this new railroad called for construction of another depot. (A very small building at the upper end of Burke displaying a "ticket office" sign apparently served as the CR&N depot, and a similar structure at the lower end of town may also have been used.) Now the OR&N constructed a single-story depot in lower Burke in the winter of 1890.

To keep up with its competition the NP also planned a new depot. (This was coupled with standard gauging the track.) The two-story structure they erected during the summer of 1891 was located just below the OR&N depot. It followed a typical NP design and was similar to stations at Mullan, Saltese, and Iron Mountain.

Along with the new NP depot came the end of the narrow gauge operation to Burke. The plan to standard gauge it had been considered for a number of years, and now that the NP line was complete to Missoula, the rails were spread from Wallace to Burke. This job was done by the end of 1891 — the grade having been widened the previous summer.

Eastern Washington State Historical Society

Engines such as this 2-6-0 were used infrequently on the Coeur d'Alene Branch as they were quite light for the steep grades. Nevertheless this photograph shows engine No. 401 pulling what is believed to be the Burke local ca. 1920.

The Mammoth and Standard mills in 1907. These mills, rated at 400 tons capacity, were later purchased by the Federal Mining & Smelting Company.

The Standard Mill just above Wallace near the mouth of Canyon Creek with an ore train unloading ore brought down canyon from the Standard Mine. The Mammoth Mill appears on the left.

Another later view of the Granite Mill showing the NP standard gauge track on the left (the narrow gauge was now gone) and the OR&N track on the right. The mill did not operate long after this.

The Gem Mill just below the town of Gem (mill owned by the Milwaukee Mining Company). This later became the site of the Hecla Mill. Note the CR&N track to the right of the UP boxcar.

Hecla Mill in 1912. Ore from the Hecla Mine in Burke is brought down canyon and dropped at the mill from cars on the "high line" behind the mill. The OWR&N track runs in front of the mill.

Barnard-Stockbridge Collection
University of Idaho Library

Gem in 1902 looking up canyon. The NP track runs in the street and the OR&N track to the right. The line branching off to the right downhill is the "high line" to the Hecla Mill. All three of these lines had four percent grades. Note the many outhouses over Canyon Creek.

Barnard-Stockbridge Collection
University of Idaho Library

Close quarters. NP engine No. 94 and an automobile passing at Gem in 1919.

Barnard-Stockbridge Collection
University of Idaho Library

Coming or going the fit was still tight. This rear view of engine No. 94 shows the tender equiped with a wooden pilot which helped it back down the canyon from Burke as there was no way to turn an engine there.

Barnard-Stockbridge Collection
University of Idaho Library

The Helena-Frisco Mill above Gem ca. 1892-1893. The narrow gauge track had been replaced by the NP standard gauge in the foreground. This mill was blown up during the labor violence known as the "Coeur d'Alene Mining War of 1892."

Early view of the San Francisco (Frisco) Mill. The track is narrow gauge and the boxcar on the left is No. 4 of the CR&N.

Black Bear in 1910. The small building on the left by the NP track is a powder house. Looking up canyon in the distance the Mammoth Mill is visible.

The Illustrated History of North Idaho
Idaho Historical Society
Standard Mill below Mace pre-1902. The
OR&N engine in the lower left corner is
spotting ore cars which are being loaded
at the ore bin.

Barnard-Stockbridge Collection
University of Idaho Library
The ore bin for the Standard Mine and
OR&N cars being loaded. These ballast
cars were frequently used to carry ore.
The year 1912.

Barnard-Stockbridge Collection
University of Idaho Library
The original Standard Mine high on the
hillside above Canyon Creek with the
tram connecting it with the ore bin.

Robert Pearson Collection
Courtesy of R.V. Nixon

The Burke local headed by engine No. 93 somewhere
in the canyon below Burke.

the same time using the most foul and disgusting language. Conductor Ed Brown stopped the unseemly quarrel as soon as possible, but not before they had disfigured each other considerably. This is the second case of the kind of occurring in a passenger coach within two weeks, and it is a matter of regret that no arrests were made.

In spite of "progress" this was still a wild frontier and not soon to change.

Following their initial construction, improvements in railroads serving Burke were infrequent. Sometime after the turn of the century the two lines agreed to share the NP rails through the center of Burke and thus eliminated that part of the duplicate parallel track. Also about this time a switchback line was constructed to serve the Hecla Mill, and the NP track was extended under the Tiger Hotel for 800 feet to the Hercules ore platform (this was completed in March, 1906).

Even though the pioneer narrow gauge had left Burke, many things were still the same. Conductor Ed Brown (of narrow gauge fame) was soon in the newspapers again, this time on the NP standard gauge to Burke. The *Coeur d'Alene Miner* of March 18, 1893 carried the story.

Several changes in depots also took place. About 1910 the OR&N depot was replaced with a two-story building of a standard UP design. This new depot, just north of its predecessor, did not last long for on July 13, 1923, a fire destroyed it, the NP station, the Hecla

A disgraceful row occurred in the coach just as the Northern Pacific train was leaving for Burke Thursday evening. Two men fought furiously in the presence of not less than a dozen ladies, at

F.J. Haynes Foundation Collection
Montana Historical Society

The narrow gauge was gone from the main street of Burke when this photograph was taken in May, 1893. And although a locomotive appears to be switching behind a distant boxcar, the crowd (including a man "tipping" a bottle on the public street — just left of track at center) seems far more interested in watching the photographer.

Barnard-Stockbridge Collection
University of Idaho Library

Tiger-Poorman mills at Burke looking down canyon 1906. The Tiger is at right and the Poorman on the left. Also at the left is the "high line" switchback serving the Hecla Mill.

Barnard-Stockbridge Collection
University of Idaho Library

Burke looking up canyon ca. 1910. The building in the center is the famous Tiger Hotel with the railroad track running through it. The track was put through it in 1906 to reach the Hercules ore bin and to allow the "high line" switchback to the Hecla. Most of the buildings to the left and above the Tiger Hotel were part of the Hercules.

Idaho Historical Society

This second OR&N (OWR&N) depot was built about 1910. It was constructed a little further up canyon than the one it replaced and followed a standard design of the UP. It is not clear why the original depot was replaced. Perhaps it was damaged by flooding or was just too small for the needs.

Mill, and most of Burke as well. Following the fire the UP constructed a new two-story depot that was also used by the NP. That building survived until 1963 when it was damaged by a flood and subsequently razed.

Passenger service between Wallace and Burke was provided mainly by the NP, but for six or seven years beginning about 1912 the OWR&N also competed for the fares. One interesting aspect of this NP service was the Saturday night train (discontinued July 21, 1926) to bring the miners into Wallace. On at least one gala occasion (February, 1924), this train was held in Wallace until 9:50 P.M. so Canyon Creek residents could

Barnard-Stockbridge Collection
University of Idaho Library

The UP Burke depot built after the July 13, 1923, fire destroyed the town. The Hecla Mill appears behind the depot.

Robert Pearson Collection
Courtesy of R. V. Nixon

NP engine No. 41 a 2-8-0 facing up canyon in Burke. The UP depot is around the corner to the left ca. 1940s.

SPOKANE, WALLACE AND BURKE

No. 22 Daily	15-20-18 Daily	13-18-22 Daily	Miles	STATIONS	21-17-14 Daily	17-19-16 Daily	No. 21 Daily
12.40	......	12.40	92	Lv... WALLACE ...Ar	......	2.15	......
f......	......	f......	96	..... Gem	......	f......	......
f......	......	......		..... Frisco	......	f......	......
f......	......	f......	97	..... Mace	......	f......	......
1.15	......	1.15	99	Ar... Burke Lv	......	1.20	......

The OWR&N only offered passenger service to Burke for a few years. This timetable from June 22, 1913, has been edited to show only service between Wallace and Burke.

see the *Hunchback of Notre Dame* at the Grande Theatre.

As with many other passenger runs, automobiles and buses began cutting into the Burke traffic, so in the spring of 1923 the NP talked of discontinuing service. Regular runs lasted until December, and at that time the Board of Trade proposed a plan to save the service. This was tried for several months with little success then dropped early in 1924.

Another mutual effort (like the joint depot) was made by the NP and UP in 1938 when the UP granted trackage rights to the NP between Wallace and Burke. The 6.23 miles of abandoned NP track to Burke was then removed in 1939.

Today, although still operated by the UP, the Burke branch is in very bad repair and its future is uncertain.

Nine Mile Canyon

Another canyon that was an early candidate for a branch railroad was Nine Mile. This canyon and its creek joined the South Fork from the north at the

R. V. Nixon Photo

UP No. 753 running extra from Wallace to Burke April 17, 1946. This Baldwin 2-8-0 was built in 1907.

R. V. Nixon Photo

No. 753 approaching the UP depot at Burke April 17, 1946.

R. V. Nixon Photo

UP depot on left with the Hecla Mill behind No. 753, April 17, 1946.

WALLACE AND BURKE

BURKE BRANCH TABLE NUMBER **44**

286 Sat. only	284 D'ly	282 Ex. Sun.	280 Ex. Sun.	Miles	(Pacific Time)	279 Ex. Sun.	281 Ex. Sun.	283 D'ly	285 Sat. only
9 45	4 40	12 25	8 00	0	Lv......Wallace......Ar	9 20	1 45	6 00	10 55
9 55	4 50	12 35	8 10	4	.........Gem.........	9 05	1 30	5 45	10 40
10 05	4 55	12 40	8 15	5	.........Dorn.........	8 58	1 23	5 38	10 33
10 20	5 20	1 05	8 40	7	Ar.......Burke.......Lv	8 50	1 15	5 30	10 25

NP service to Burke was at its height when this timetable was issued on August 1, 1917.

R.V. Nixon Photo

Above the UP depot (on the left) No. 753 contends the right-of-way with that apparition — the automobile, April 17, 1946.

lower end of Wallace near the site of the NP depot.

The first claims were located in the Nine Mile area in 1884 by none other than A. J. Prichard and his party. These were followed in 1885 by O. B. Wallace's (son of Colonel Wallace) Black Cloud claim.

The Granite mine was the first big producer in the Nine Mile, but surpris-ingly its shipments were loaded on CR&N cars at the Granite Mill on lower Canyon Creek Canyon. Because of rail transportation on Canyon Creek, the Granite Mine constructed a tram to carry its ore over the ridge between the two creeks. Its mill was the first to ship ore by rail from east of Wardner. That ship-ment of only 13 tons was the start of an early success. (The mine's name was later changed to the Success.) The Gra-nite was soon one of the biggest ship-pers from Canyon Creek. Its success and work on other mines in Nine Mile Can-yon soon drew the interest of the NP.

In August of 1888, before its takeover of the CR&N, the NP had surveyors, led by J. O. Maxon, working in Nine Mile. By October they had laid out a switch-back line as far as Murray Pass and con-nected with another NP survey from Thompson Falls, Montana. However, actual construction was not yet started.

Local citizens' hopes for this branch rose in the spring when the rival OR&N also started a survey there. This did prompt the NP to grade half a mile and to lay several hundred yards of track,

Barnard-Stockbridge Collection
University of Idaho Library

The Rex Mill at Bradyville (also known as Sunset) at the end of track in Nine Mile Canyon. The NP also ran a short extention of track on a switchback up the east fork of the creek. This mill (shown here in 1906) was connected with its mine by an aerial tram.

but work came to a halt when a mine owner with property in the path of the railroad refused to let the line cross his claim. This refusal held the line up for a number of years.

Most of the mine owners in the canyon desperately wanted the railroad as the case of the California Mine demonstrated. In the spring of 1890 its owners shipped the first ore from Nine Mile in crude state on three sleds. The ore was unloaded at the OR&N depot at Wallace by shoveling it onto the platform and then into boxcars. While sledding was possible about 32 tons of ore were moved each day, but the owners claimed another 20 tons could be put out if the railroad was built.

A little later that spring the NP had a new railroad incorporated to build up Nine Mile from Wallace to the Sunset mines. The Wallace & Sunset Railroad (W&S) filed articles on April 15, 1890, with capital stock of $500,000. George W. Dickinson (assistant manager of NP in Helena), Patrick Clark, Charles S.

Sunset, Idaho.

376

Photo by Barnard's Studio.

Another view of the end of track in Nine Mile looking up canyon. The Rex Mill is behind the trees in the center. Note the large collection of mine timbers in the foreground.

Warren, Cary D. Porter, and John A. Finch were the incorporators. This new corporation was necessary because NP lawyers discovered that the old CR&N charter did not include possible routes up side canyons.

The W&S graded about five miles out of Wallace during the summer of 1890 with the work progressing very slowly. Some of the men working were transferred to the NP construction near Lookout. By the end of the year grading had reached the East Fork with about $46,000 having been spent. The plans were to lay track in the spring. The OR&N also started grading in the canyon in 1890, but this work didn't go far and track was never laid.

When the spring of 1891 arrived the dispute over the right-of-way across a

Dr. Philip R. Hastings Photo
UP 2-8-0 No. 737 switching the zinc plant on the remnant of the Sierra Nevada February 24, 1951.

mining claim surfaced again. While this alone could have been enough to keep the rail from being laid, another greater obstacle arose. The Sunset mines contracted with the UP (OR&N) to carry their entire output for one year, thus frustrating tracklaying even further.

The exact year NP tracklaying was carried out is unclear. It appears this work was finally done about the turn of the century. Just why it took this long is up to speculation. It appears that the reasons were probably those previously mentioned as well as the NP's poor financial condition.

The rails were laid up Nine Mile to the site of Sunset, later called Bradyville. From there a switchback line ran a short distance up the East Fork. At Sunset the branch served the Rex Mill which was supplied by an aerial tram. This mill was later owned by the Tamarack-Custer Consolidated. In addition to these a number of other mines in the canyon were also served.

In 1934 the 2.27 miles of track between Sunset and Bunn were abandoned and taken up. (This was probably due in part to the great flood of 1933.) The W&S branch was terminated when the last portion of track between Bunn and Wallace was removed in 1968.

The Sierra Nevada Branch

The first branch constructed in the Coeur d'Alenes by the OR&N was the Sierra Nevada Branch. This five-mile spur left the main track near Sweeny (later called Bradley — site of the Empire State-Idaho Concentrator) and climbed a maximum four percent grade to the Sierra Nevada Mine at the head of Deadwood Gulch. Construction was begun in the fall of 1900 by Miller & Welch, contractors from St. Paul, Minnesota, and finished in the spring of

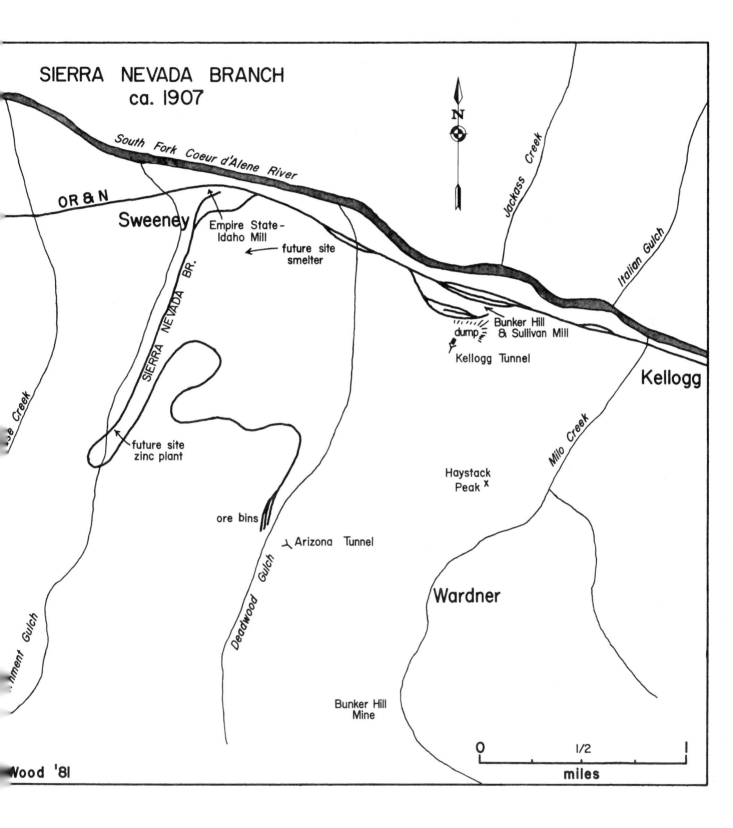

SIERRA NEVADA BRANCH
ca. 1907

South Fork Coeur d'Alene River

OR & N

Sweeney

Empire State-
Idaho Mill

future site
smelter

SIERRA NEVADA BR.

future site
zinc plant

ore bins

Arizona Tunnel

Deadwood Gulch

Bunker Hill
Mine

N

Jackass Creek

Italian Gulch

dump

Bunker Hill
& Sullivan Mill

Kellogg Tunnel

Kellogg

Milo Creek

Haystack
Peak X

Wardner

0   1/2

miles

Wood '81

Empire State ore bin at the top of the Sierra Nevada Branch of the OR&N. The grade (downhill to the right) was a steady four percent.

1901. To legally construct the branch the Idaho Extensions Company (the OR&N subsidiary which had built the line) had to file supplementary articles of incorporation in its home state of Oregon.

In 1923 the Bunker Hill and Sullivan constructed its zinc plant on the lower part of the line. Luckily this provided the branch a new source of traffic, for the rails to the Sierra Nevada Mine itself became unnecessary as the minerals played out and new tunnels were opened. Thus in 1941 the line was shorted to 3.24 miles, and in 1953 it was further reduced to its current two-mile length.

The Idaho Northern Railroad

The North Fork of the Coeur d'Alene

The Bunker Hill & Sullivan zinc plant under construction April 14, 1927. The train near the bottom of the construction is heading up the Sierra Nevada Branch. Then loops back off to the right and passes above the new plant. Note the cut on the hillside to the left.

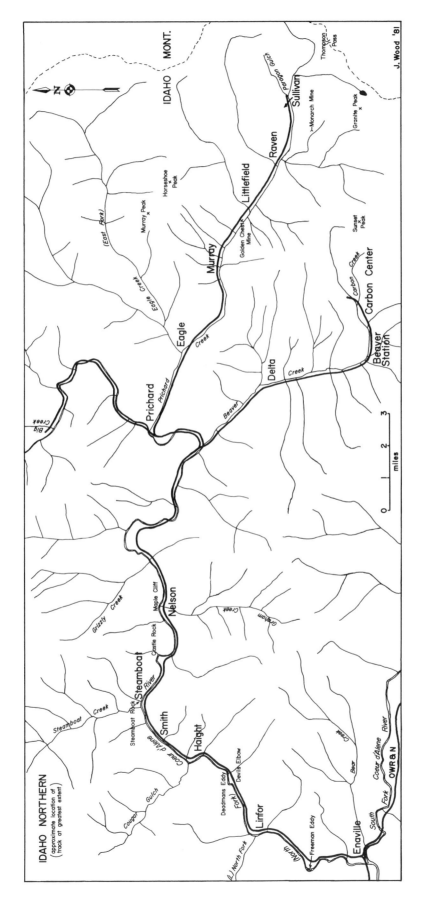

River had spawned the initial excitement in the Coeur d'Alenes, but the easy money in gold had played out by the time the first railroad was constructed. The CR&N bypassed the North Fork and it was not until years later that a line was constructed there.

The earliest rumors of a North Fork line were in the spring of 1889 when the OR&N considered it as the only feasible route to reach the lead-silver mines in the Sunset area. (This was the area later served by the Wallace & Sunset branch of the NP up Nine Mile Canyon.) But these rumors failed to result in any action, and the project languished for nearly ten more years.

In November of 1898 the Idaho Northern Railroad (IN) was incorporated in Idaho to build from the mouth of the Coeur d'Alene River up to the North Fork and then up the North Fork and Prichard Creek past the town of Murray to the headwaters of Bear Gulch. A branch line was also to be built up Beaver Creek and then up to the head of Carbon Creek. The capital stock was $2,500,000 with the main office in Boise. The incorporators were W. Thomas Hart of Weiser (president), Bamford Robb of Portland, Joseph Perrault, Alfred Eoff, and Bamford A. Robb of Boise. (It is interesting to note that another railroad with the same name had been incorporated to operate in southern Idaho the previous January. That line later became part of the Oregon Short Line and then UP. It had absolutely no connection with this line in North Idaho.)

Surveys for the IN were reportedly completed in the spring of 1899, but again the effort stalled. Apparently it was very difficult to get investors interested in the project.

The ice was finally broken in 1906

when B. F. O'Neill, the president of the Wallace State Bank of Commerce, threw all his power behind the project. He was also able to sell construction bonds to the OR&N, and it appeared that the railroad ultimately invested over $1,500,000 in the IN through O'Neill's urging.

Bids for construction of the 33 miles between Enaville (on the OR&N line) and Paragon Gulch (six miles above Murray) were opened on August 15, 1907, and the winner was the Pacific Coast Construction Company of Portland. Some grading was done before year's end, but work wasn't pushed due to a financial panic in the fall. In June of 1908 the construction crew was increased to 1,200 men to handle the work of removing more than 300,000 cubic yards of rock. The resulting line was to have easy curves and grades the entire 33 miles from Enaville to Paragon Gulch.

In the fall of 1908 E. P. Spaulding, vice-president and general manager of the Idaho Northern, described the progress of the line.

The first six miles of the road, including the stations at Enaville, Little North Fork and Haights, have been opened for handling freight on work trains. Stations at Smith's Spur and Steamboat Creek will be opened in a few weeks: Nelson siding, November 1; Beaver, November 15; Prichard and Eagle, December 1. Murray will be reached and operation started by December 15, and Raven, Monarch and Paragon by the first of the year. The grade between Enaville and the mouth of Prichard Creek will be finished within 30 days. Grading beyond Prichard Creek is about half done and will be completed early in November. Track on four miles has been laid and the work is progressing at a rate of from a half to three-quarters of a mile a day. Work is being done on both of the bridges across the north fork of the Coeur d'Alene River, each to be about 150 feet long. One is 16 miles above Enaville and the other about 19 miles. The officers of the company are: B. F. O'Neill of Wallace president; E. P. Spaulding of Spokane vice president and general manager, and E. L.

Proebsting of Wallace secretary and treasurer. W. P. Smith is chief engineer.

Construction to Murray was finished in 1908, and the first train, a special from Wallace carrying over 150 people arrived there the afternoon of December thirtieth. Adam Aulbach, an early newspaper editor, presided over the festivities of the day with speeches by O'Neill, Spaulding, and even D. C. Corbin.

The year 1909 began with big plans for the line, for service was to be extended from Murray about five miles east to Monarch to serve the Monarch Mine, which was managed by Spauld-

ing. Branches were also planned up Beaver Creek and up the Little North Fork (the latter was never constructed).

B. F. O'Neill's dream of great ore traffic on the road never did materialize. The lead-silver mines in the area just didn't have the capacity to keep the railroad busy. On May 12, 1911, O'Neill's bank had folded and he was eventually tried and convicted for making a false bank report. One charge was "that large loans were made without security for the construction of the railroad from Enaville to Murray."

The railroad itself was taken over by the OWR&N on March 1, 1911, and op-

Don Roberts Collection
Oregon Historical Society

Idaho Northern engine No. 1. This ex-OR&N 4-4-0 (No. 87) was owned by the IN for only about two years until the line was taken over by the OWR&N.

Don Roberts Collection
Oregon Historical Society

Idaho Northern No. 2 (a 2-8-0) heading a passenger train. The location of this former OR&N engine (No. 161) was probably Murray.

erated as the Idaho Northern Branch. The line struggled on, and in 1916 construction of the long proposed ten-mile branch up Beaver Creek was commenced at the urging of the Ray-Jefferson Mine which had struck a new zinc vein. Twohy Brothers of Portland

Idaho Historical Society

OWR&N depot at Murray on the Idaho Northern Branch.

were awarded the contract, and active work was underway by October first on 125,000 cubic yards of grading and other constructions with the cost estimated at $200,000. The branch opened to the mill at a 3,200-foot elevation in February, 1917. But again the ore traffic didn't materialize for one month later the Ray-Jefferson closed the mill due to insufficient ore.

The year 1917 did see one very interesting load pass over the railroad. Gold mining still continued on Prichard Creek, and toward that end a large dredge was imported from the Klondike. Dredge No. 9 had been constructed by the Yuba Construction Company of Marysville, California, with Bucyrus machinery and assembled in the Klondike in 1911. The hull was 44 feet wide, 105 feet long, and eight feet deep. The dredge operated on Eldorado Creek for the Yukon Gold Company five years

Idaho Northern No. 1 (here still numbered for the OR&N) hauls the first ore shipment over the line from the Black Horse Mine. The location was the end of track at Paragon.

then was dismantled and shipped to Murray, the last leg of the journey being on the IN.

A track washout close to Murray in December of 1917 caused the first abandonment of the line when the 11.3 mile portion between Prichard and Paragon was dropped the following year.

The main traffic on the railroad was now log hauling. Several companies including McGoldrick Lumber and Rose Lake Lumber shipped over the line, and several independent logging spurs were constructed. The Mountain Lumber Company built one of these spurs using the old IN track from Prichard up

The gold dredge at Murray brought in over the Idaho Northern line.

WALLACE, ENAVILLE, MURRAY AND MONARCH

Nos. 23-98 Mixed Daily	Miles	TABLE No. 11	Elevation	Nos. 97-24 Mixed Daily	
.... 12 05	0	Lv.........WALLACE.........Ar	2745	9 15	....
.... 12 20	4	........Osborne............	2539	8 55	....
.... 12 40	11	........Wardner............	2304	8 35	....
f.........	13	......Sweeney.............		f.........	....
.... 1 05	18	........Enaville...........	2137	8 15	....
f.........	22	....Little North Fork.........	2163	f.........	....
f.........	25	........Haights............	2182	f.........	....
f.........	27	......Smith's Spur..........	2198	f.........	....
f 1 35	29	.....Steamboat.............	2215	6 35	....
1 50	33	........Nelson.............	2261	6 10	....
2 10	39	........Beaver.............	2232	5 50	....
2 30	44	........Waite.............	2371	5 35	....
2 50	48	........Murray.............	2502	5 20	....
f.........		........Raven.............	2724		....
3 20	56	Ar......Monarch.........Lv	3331	5 00	....

This OWR&N timetable of September 7, 1912, shows service to Monarch which was only one mile from the end of the line at Paragon.

The remains of the Idaho Northern after the great flood of 1933. The line was scrapped after this.

Prichard Creek to Eagle Creek. The spur then followed Eagle Creek and its east fork for a total of 11 miles.

In 1923 the Idaho Northern Branch itself was also extended about ten miles further up the North Fork from Prichard to Big Creek (later called Shoshone Creek). This aided logging and was also aimed at developing some copper prospects in that area.

But the railroad never did carry any great amount of traffic. The construction of a U.S. Forest Service road along the North Fork and the logging trucks it brought doomed the line. When the terrible flooding which affected the whole area in December of 1933 washed out nearly all the track, the OWR&N applied to the Interstate Commerce Commission to abandon the line.

Today much of the old roadbed serves as the state highway which carries numerous hunters, fishermen, and tourists along this beautiful waterway that was the scene of the first "rush" to the Coeur d'Alenes.

The Pine Creek Branch

Pine Creek is a tributary of the South Fork of the Coeur d'Alene River. It enters the river from the south at a point about two miles upstream from Kingston and about six miles below Kellogg.

Many claims were located on Pine Creek during the rush to the South Fork, but little work was done there until after 1910 because the ore contained a high percentage of zinc, and was therefore difficult to process. Nevertheless, the Highland-Surprise and Constitution mines came to be two of the most important in the area.

The OWR&N served the mines in the area from Pine Creek station at the mouth of the creek, and in 1912 a $30,000 profit from the Highland-

Surprise encouraged the *Wallace Miner* to discuss the need for a branch line and the OWR&N plans to build one. But no action was taken by the railroad until 1917. In that year surveys were made up Pine Creek to the Highland-Surprise and Constitution mines. Grading was begun in the fall, but stopped in 1918 after only a few miles were completed and no rails laid. Mining activity, which had picked up due to the railroad construction, now suffered. The Anaconda Copper Company had leased the Douglas Mine in 1917, but now they dropped the property.

In 1923 excitement over a railroad in the area revived. The OWR&N finally laid the track on about two miles of the previously completed grade, to Heim Ranch, and on August 30, 1923, the *Wallace Miner* reported that a private company called the North Side Railroad planned to build further up Pine Creek. The President of the company, a Mr. Patrick Burke, claimed construction would begin the following week. This line was to add another two miles to the OWR&N spur. The resulting line would reach Masonia and the loading bins to be built there. The North Side Railroad was also in negotiations with the OWR&N to haul the ore over its two miles of proposed track as well as the OWR&N's existing two miles.

For some reason this extension was not built, and in 1925 the UP sent a Dr. Albert Boyle to this area to see if the mining potential warranted extending their own line. The decision was apparently adverse as no more action was taken.

Finally in 1934 the spur itself was removed and the Pine Creek Branch (such as it was) disappeared.

The Coeur d'Alene & Spokane Railway

The Coeur d'Alene & Spokane Railway Company Limited (C&S), more commonly called "the electric line" by the local inhabitants, played an important role in service to the Coeur d'Alenes and cannot be overlooked. However, as it made no physical connection with the mines, and since its scope was far wider than just their service, coverage of this interesting line has been purposely kept brief.

The C&S was incorporated in Idaho October 20, 1902, by lumberman F. A. Blackwell and Ambrose Bettes. Construction was completed and the line opened for business on December 28, 1903. The line was built as an electric interurban to connect Spokane, Washington and Coeur d'Alene, Idaho, with frequent service (this became hourly during the busiest years). The morning train to Coeur d'Alene, which provided connections with the Red Collar Line steamers, was known as the Shoshone Flyer (the mining area was in Shoshone County). The steamers (the finest being the *Georgie Oakes*) crossed Coeur d'Alene Lake to Harrison. At Harrison passengers could board the OR&N train and complete the trip to the mining area.

Eastern Washington State Historical Society
Billboard ad promoting service to Wallace from Spokane over the electric line and the Red Collar steamers to Harrison.

This route to the mines was much shorter and therefore less time consuming than the route of the OR&N which swung far out of the way to the south reaching the town of Tekoa before it turned northeast and headed back toward the southern end of Coeur d'Alene Lake. With its shorter route the C&S and the Red Collar Line managed to win thousands of dollars in passenger fares from the OR&N. Eventually the OR&N countered this challenge by constructing the Amwaco Branch (the next line covered) which was completed in 1910.

While the C&S lost much of its traffic to the mines due to the Amwaco Branch, it still managed for some years to carry on a brisk passenger business to Coeur d'Alene and other points. Nevertheless the line went through several owners and name changes. It had become part

The first passengers over the Coeur d'Alene & Spokane electric line to Post Falls, Idaho, on the way to Coeur d'Alene October 24, 1902. A steam engine is used at this time as the electric wire was not yet installed.

Lefler Photo
Marvin Jones Collection
The Coeur d'Alene Express in Coeur
d'Alene with the lake in the background
— the year 1910.

Libby Photo
Museum of North Idaho
The OWR&N steamboat *Harrison* made connections between Amwaco and Harrison across Coeur d'Alene Lake.
This view was taken in 1924 at the Campfire Girls camp.

of the Inland Empire Railway Co. in 1906, which after bankruptcy in 1919 was reorganized as the Inland Empire Railroad. In 1927 the Great Northern purchased the line and called it the Spokane, Coeur d'Alene and Palouse. Under this ownership electrics continued to carry passengers to Coeur d'Alene until 1940.

Today portions of "the electric line" still survive as part of the BN freight line to Coeur d'Alene but they offer little to remind one of the Shoshone Flyer and the service it once provided.

The Amwaco Branch

As just related the C&S electric line managed to lure many passengers from the OR&N route between Spokane and the mines. Faced with this loss of fares, a new railroad was proposed.

On July 26, 1906, the Lake Creek & Coeur d'Alene Railroad was incorporated in Oregon to build "a line from Lockwood, Washington, on the main line OR&N 21.8 miles southeast of Spokane, west to a point on Lake Coeur d'Alene near Farmington Landing 12.36 miles. From this point the company will operate boats to Harrison, Idaho, which is also on the OR&N." The president of the company was J. P. O'Brien and the chief engineer George W. Boschke of Portland, Oregon.

In May of 1909 Twohy Brothers of Spokane won the contract to construct the line. The work was described as "moderately heavy. Maximum curves 10° and maximum grade eastbound 1.7%, westbound 1.5%."

The work was completed and the new line opened on June 12, 1910. Track left the main line OR&N at Lake Junction (later called Bell), Washington, and followed Lake Creek to a terminal at Lake Point, Idaho, at the head of Windy Bay

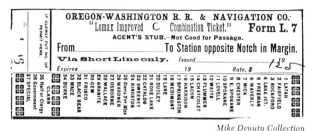

Mike Denuty Collection

This OWR&N ticket on the Wallace Branch was issued November 27, 1911. It was sold to a rider for passage between Bell, Washington, and Plummer, Idaho — cost $1.25.

on Coeur d'Alene Lake. The dock at the head of the bay was too shallow in times of low water, so track was quickly extended along the east side of the bay to a new terminal known as Amwaco where the water was deeper. The new length of the line was 14.18 miles.

The Lake Creek & Coeur d'Alene was operated by the OR&N and never owned its own equipment. On December 23, 1910, shortly after the start of operations, it was absorbed by the newly formed OWR&N. This new company constructed the steamboat *Harrison* to provide transportation for the six-mile trip across the lake from Amwaco to Harrison. This new route was about 25 miles shorter than the previous line through Tekoa. Two trains a day operated over the branch and it soon became so popular that the *Harrison* was able to win back $80,000 a year in traffic from the Red Collar Line.

In the early 1920s passenger traffic over the branch stopped when the OWR&N made an agreement with the Chicago, Milwaukee, St. Paul & Pacific

20- Daily	18- Daily	Mls.	BETWEEN BELL AND HARRISON	17- Daily	19- Daily		Table 85.
3.05	8.35		Lv........Spokane......Ar.	11.30	6.00	.....	.....
3.55	9.26	0	Lv..........Bell.......Ar.	10.45	5.15		
4.30	10.00	14	Ar. ....Amwaco ......Lv.	10.05	4.35		
			via Steamer "Harrison"				
5.05	10.25	20	Ar ......Harrison...... Lv.	9.30	4.10	.....	.....

A 1914 UP timetable showing service over the Amwaco line to Harrison.

to use the Milwaukee track between Manito and Plummer. Like the Amwaco Branch this arrangement cut off the out-of-the-way trip through Tekoa, but in addition it also eliminated the need to transfer passengers and freight for the trip over Coeur d'Alene Lake.

Although its passenger service was discontinued, the Amwaco Branch was operated as a freight line handling sand, gravel, wheat, and timber until the line was abandoned in 1932.

The Morning Mine Railroad

The Morning Mine Railroad (later known as the Larson & Greenough Railroad) was unique in the Coeur d'Alenes. It was the only private steam railroad transporting ore from the mine shaft to the concentrator. A few other mines did use common carrier railroads or electric railroads for this kind of service, but even this was rare. The most common method of transporting ore between a

tunnel entrance and a mill that were far apart was the use of a cable and bucket tramway. Many mines such as the Bunker Hill and the Granite had used cable trams with varying degrees of success. In fact the Morning Mine itself used a cable early in its operations.

The early tunnel entrances of the Morning were located about 1½ miles up Mill Creek to the north of Mullan on a very steep hillside. Charles Hussy bought the claim in 1887 and made extensive improvements including a 2¼-mile tram to connect the mine and a 250-ton mill which was built about half a mile downstream (west) from Mullan.

The cable tram, completed in 1889, soon became a cause of great frustration as well as financial loss. In less than a year the cable had to be completely replaced, and even after that continued to breakdown. When the mine was sold at the end of 1891 to a Milwaukee syndicate, one of the first changes the new

Washington State University Library

This first mill of the Morning Mine just below Mullan was connected by aerial tram to the mine up the hill to the left. Two narrow gauge flatcars of the CR&N are visible in front of the mill. This mill was replaced when the narrow gauge line of the Morning Mine was built.

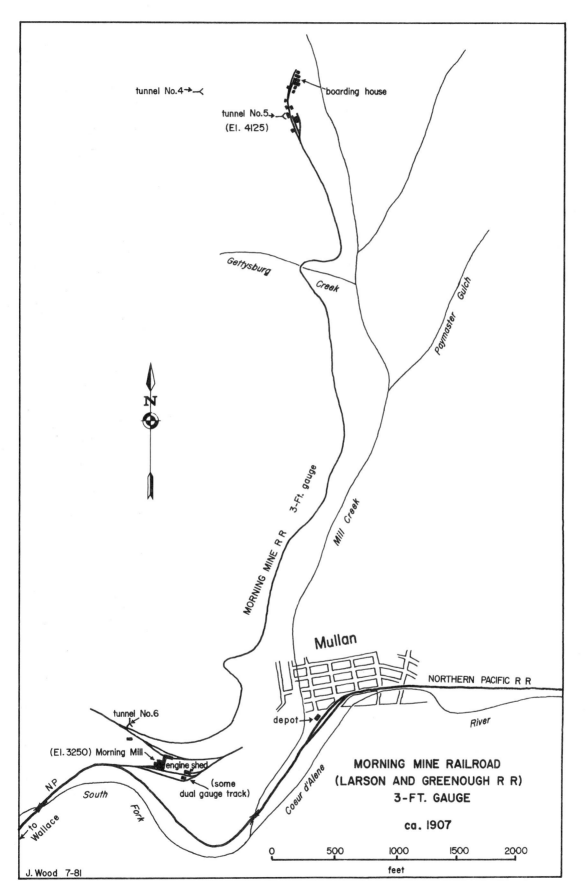

tunnel No.4 →⤙

boarding house

tunnel No.5 →⤙
(El. 4125)

Gettysburg

Creek

Paymaster Gulch

N

MORNING MINE R R 3-Ft. gauge

Mill Creek

Mullan

NORTHERN PACIFIC R R

depot →

River

tunnel No.6

(El. 3250) Morning Mill
engine shed

(some
dual gauge track)

NP

South

Fork

to
Wallace

Coeur d'Alene

MORNING MINE RAILROAD
(LARSON AND GREENOUGH R R)
3-FT. GAUGE

ca. 1907

0   500   1000   1500   2000

feet

J. Wood 7-81

owners made was the elimination of the long tram.

In its place a three-foot gauge railroad was planned. The right-of-way for this line was secured in June of 1892, and about 200 men were put to work on its construction. The line started at a new 600-ton mill constructed near the old one below Mullan. The mill was served by both the NP and OR&N. The Morning Railroad left the mill and made numerous switchbacks up the hillside before following Mill Creek 3¼ miles to the end of the line at a new ore bin. A short tramway connected this ore bin with the No. 4 tunnel of the Morning Mine which was about 500 feet higher in elevation. The railroad had a nearly continuous seven percent grade and included two curves of 60 degrees.

Ordinary steam engines would have found the challenge of the grade and curves of this line insurmountable, but the geared Shay locomotive that was put to work when the line opened during the winter of 1892 overcame them. Even snow three to five feet in depth was unable to stop the engine and its plow. The *Coeur d'Alene Miner* (February 18,

1893) acclaimed its prowess, "The engine weighs 19 tons and is a veritable little giant, as it can haul over forty tons up the grade."

The engineer, F. Thatcher, must have had quite a job bringing the loads down the seven percent grade in the ice and snow, especially as the locomotive was equipped with old-style steam brakes! The conditions in the winter did limit the trains downgrade to fifty tons, or five cars. At this time the operating equipment consisted of eight dump cars of ten tons capacity.

Operations were not totally devoid of trouble. In January of 1893 the locomotive and several cars jumped the track and probably would have rolled hundreds of feet to the bottom of the hill, but fortunately they had gone off on the uphill side. Later in March, when the locomotive-operated plow had dug a deep trench and crews had resorted to hand shoveling, the heavy snowfall was finally able to blockade the line.

The next month as efforts were being made to reopen the line, the *Coeur d'Alene Miner* (April 29, 1893) again

Barnard-Stockbridge Collection
University of Idaho Library
The second Morning Concentrator was built at the foot of the hill. The switchbacks of the narrow gauge line can be seen above the mill. The original mill appears on the lower right.

found occasion to praise the Shay engine.

The little Morning engine was upon the hill today, this being her first appearance for several weeks. It looks good to see her out, although the occasion was not the immediate resumption of operations at the mine.

By the way, our diminutive locomotive is a hummer. She's little, but she's the loudest thing in this precinct. [This was a reference to the loud, rapid exhaust due to the Shay's low gearing and three cylinders.] We all take pride in her, just the same.

As operations resumed, runs up the hill and back quickened. The best performance was 50 minutes starting with five empties at the mill, hauling them up to the mine, loading them, and returning to the mill.

But the light-hearted mood of record attempts was soon to disappear in the gloom of the 1893 panic. Like so many other businesses the Morning Mine also fell into receivership. The mine and the railroad remained idle through 1894, and forest fires that summer caused some damage to the track.

In 1895 the Morning Mine and railroad were sold to Peter Larsen of Helena, Montana, and Thomas L.

Greenough of Missoula, Montana. (Now the railroad was called the Larsen and Greenough Railroad.) In addition the new owners also acquired the You Like Mine which they worked in connection with the Morning. One of their first projects was the construction of a new tunnel, known as tunnel No. 5, which was hundreds of feet lower than the mouth of tunnel No. 4. The mouth of the new tunnel would be low enough for ore to be dumped directly into the narrow gauge cars instead of using the short tram necessary with the previous tunnel.

The next event at the Morning was a fire on April 17, 1898, which destroyed the mill at the bottom of the hill, but by August fifteenth a new mill was completed at the old site.

Production of the Morning combined with the You Like was so great by 1904 that it exceeded that of the Bunker Hill and Sullivan. But even before this, starting in 1900, construction was begun on a new tunnel that would exit just above the mill, 830 feet below the No. 5 tunnel. This new No. 6 tunnel would eliminate the need for the narrow gauge

P. E. Percy Collection

Larson & Greenough engine No. 1 (Shay construction number 538) on the Morning Mine Railroad three-foot gauge. The engine was pushing eight ore cars of ten ton capacity up the seven percent grade on a 60 degree curve. The year 1897.

railroad. While this railroad was considered very efficient and quite economical (in 1905 it was estimated to have carried 1,000 tons per day at less than ten cents per ton including hauling timbers and other supplies), the new tunnel would eliminate even this bother and expense.

By 1906 the No. 6 tunnel was completed and the narrow gauge railroad abandoned. Thus ended the history of a very unique part of the railroad history in the Coeur d'Alenes. However, even today the grade of this line can be seen on the hillside above Mullan.

The Amador Railway

The Amador Railway might rightfully be considered outside the scope of this book as it was wholly in Montana and east of the Coeur d'Alene Mining Area, but as it was nearby and its only connection to the outside world was the Coeur d'Alene Branch of the NP, it has been

included. Also the fact that this line was one of the quaintest in the area played strongly in its favor.

The Amador Railway was built in Montana on Cedar Creek, the site of a mining area even older than that of the Coeur d'Alenes. Cedar Creek flowed into the Clark Fork River at Iron Mountain, which was on the south side of the river across from Superior. The early gold rush in the area had died down by the time the railroad was considered and the new attraction was copper ore.

The Amador Copper Mine was discovered in 1889, but little work was done until after 1900. In 1902 the Amador Gold and Copper Mining Company operated the property. Efforts to build a railroad to serve the mine were begun and on September 1, 1904, a charter was granted in Delaware with authorized capital of one million dollars. Erasmus B. Waples of Wilmington, Delaware, and William Surlin of Carlin-

Barnard-Stockbridge Collection
University of Idaho Library
Engine No. 1 and a load of ore heading downgrade from the Morning Mine ore bins.

Morning Mine train near the mine showing the interesting Larson & Greenough ore cars complete with link-and-pin couplers.

Morning Mine buildings at the end of track in 1904. The mess hall is in the foreground with the bunkhouse just beyond. The large ore bin in the background is connected to the No. 5 tunnel of the Morning.

The Amador Mine on Cedar Creek in Montana 1902. The standard gauge Amador Railway was constructed here two years later.

Bill Pike Collection
Courtesy Mineral County Historical Book 1976
NP engine No. 585, a 2-6-0, was apparently leased by the Amador Railway. The flatcars in the photograph and several boxcars were probably all the equipment actually owned by the line. The location is the town of Amador just east of Iron Mountain, Montana. Note the ore piled directly on the flatcars.

ville, Illinois, were the directors. Apparently contracts were let which were not carried out, and in 1905 the Ross & Company of Chicago took them over. Work was finished and the first ore shipped in the spring of 1906.

The line left the Coeur d'Alene Branch of the NP at Amador City, just east of Iron Mountain, and proceeded south up Cedar Creek about 11 miles to the Amador Mine. Apparently the right-of-way was never legally secured, and the rails were just laid over the easiest path. A tiny 60-ton smelter was erected near Amador City to save the cost of shipping the crude ore over the NP to Butte.

The railroad seemingly never owned its own locomotive and leased the No. 585, a Baldwin 2-6-0, from the NP. It did own several flatcars, a handcar, and possibly several dilapidated boxcars.

The railroad operated in a very casual manner, and reportedly the priority over the line was given to packtrains that were forced to use the roadbed in many places where the canyon was too narrow for a separate road.

The line was finally abandoned in 1919 when trucks took over the job of hauling the ore. While the mine continued operations for awhile it too eventually ceased operations.

Barnard-Stockbridge Collection
University of Idaho Library
Engine facilities for the Amador Railway were very basic. This one-stall engine shed and coal dock served engine No. 585 somewhere near Iron Mountain.

Barnard-Stockbridge Collection
University of Idaho Library

The Amador Railway at the Amador Mine. Note the small "third rail" laid in the middle of the regular track. Apparently this and one other rail were used to allow small hand ore cars to be pushed down track (they would have leaned considerably due to the difference in rail height).

Potpourri

In addition to the lines already mentioned, there were numerous other industrial operations in the Coeur d'Alenes. Many mines used underground rail and storage-battery locomotives for the movement of ore (no attempt has been made to include these in this work), a few mines used aboveground lines for the movement of timbers and machinery, and many logging companies operated railroads in the surrounding forests. But one of the most extensive lines not mentioned previously is the Bunker Hill Smelter Railroad.

After a dispute with the huge American Smelting & Refining Company (the AS&R Co. had a 25-year contract to process Bunker Hill ore), the Bunker Hill constructed a smelter of its own at Kellogg. This plant was put in operation in July of 1917.

A standard gauge railroad a little less than a mile long was built to connect the mill-yard of the mine with the smelter, and additional tracks were laid around the smelter to facilitate the ore processing.

This operation ordered its first locomotive in 1916, and saw at least five steam engines come and go. The steam

Idaho Historical Society
This Caterpillar tractor, while not a locomotive, was too "cute" to pass up. It hauled ore wagons from the Tyler lease for the Bunker Hill in the early 1900s.

Alco Historic Photos
Bunker Hill Smelter engine No. 3 shown in this builder's photograph was an Alco (Cooke) 0-6-0 built in May, 1919.

engines are now long gone, but the line still carries on with diesel power.

An older and much smaller operation was that of the Standard Mine. In 1896 the Standard Mine finished its Campbell tunnel which opened near the bottom of Canyon Creek. At that time a narrow gauge railroad was constructed, but little is known about it. Photographs do show some narrow gauge track in a timber storage area near the mill, and it is likely the railroad was used to move the timbers and mining equipment.

The only record of a locomotive was the purchase of an 18-inch gauge 0-4-0 Porter engine in December of 1896. Apparently this engine operated on compressed air which was stored in what resembled a locomotive boiler. This would have allowed operation in covered areas without the danger of a combustion engine.

The line must have ceased operation at or before 1916 when the mine shut down. The little locomotive was ac-

Owens Museum
Robert Pearson Collection

Hecla Mining Company engine No. 16 was a saddle tank 0-4-0 said to have come from the Anaconda Copper Company. At the time this picture was taken, February 23, 1948, the locomotive was out of operation.

Bert Ward Collection

Hecla Mining Company engine No. 17 was a Porter 0-4-0 construction number 1715 which was originally built for the Standard Mine as a compressed air locomotive. The Hecla converted it to steamer as it appears in this photo.

quired by the Hecla Mine which also operated a similar narrow gauge railroad.

The Hecla Mine railroad was also apparently used for hauling timbers and the like above ground, but it is difficult to determine its gauge. The engine acquired from the Standard was 18-inch gauge, but another engine purchased from the Anaconda Copper Company was reportedly 24-inch gauge. As the Hecla shop performed major work on the Standard engine by converting it from compressed air to a regular steam boiler, it is probable that it was also

H. L. Broadbelt Collection

National Mining Company electric locomotive No. 1 built by Baldwin-Westinghouse in July, 1903. A photograph showing the National Mill and some of the railroad's 42-inch gauge track appears in Chapter Four.

Bill Pike Collection
Courtesy Mineral County Historical Book 1976

Iron Mountain Company 0-4-0 saddle tank Porter the "Helena" which hauled ore a short distance from the mine to this ore bin and chute which carried the ore to a tramway further down the mountain.

changed to 24-inch gauge (the apparent gauge of Hecla track). In addition to these steamers the Hecla also used several small Plymouth internal combustion engines in later years.

A couple of miles east of Mullan, just beyond the Gold Hunter Mill, was the mill of the National Mine and its two-mile electric railroad. This mine was developed sometime shortly after the turn of the century as a copper producer, but the quality of ore was so poor that it only paid to work it when the price of copper was very high. (The Snowstorm Mine further east had a much higher grade of copper ore.) Part of the development of the National Mine included an electric railroad about two miles long that ran from the mill on the NP line up Deadman Gulch to the mine. This line, believed to be 42-inch gauge, served like the Morning Mine Railroad in place of an aerial tram, but unlike the Morning Railroad which was replaced by a new tunnel, the National railroad ceased to function due to the failure of its mine (probably before the start of World War I).

Straying slightly outside the Coeur d'Alenes again (as with the Amador Railway), we pick up the little line of the Iron Mountain Mining Company across the mountains in Montana. Sometime in the 1890s the Iron Mountain Company constructed a short narrow gauge (possibly three-foot gauge) railroad to connect their mine tunnel with an ore bin at the top of a cable tram. This tram carried the ore down the steep hillside to the concentrator.

After the concentration the ore was apparently hauled by wagon the rest of the way down to the Clark Fork River and across the bridge to the town of Iron Mountain, Montana, on the Coeur d'Alene Branch of the NP. The town, as the name suggests, was founded to serve the mine.

The tiny railroad was served by a cute little Porter 0-4-0 called "The Helena." The line continued operation until the mill was shut down in 1916.

Besides these mining oriented railways, there were numerous logging railroads in the area of the Coeur d'Alenes which hauled great quantities of timber out of the woods. While it is not the intent of this work to cover logging lines, at least some mention needs to be made of them in passing.

The greatest number of logging lines in the area were located on the North Fork of the Coeur d'Alene River. The Mountain Lumber Company on Eagle Creek was already mentioned, and others in the area were Hedlund Lumber & Box, Hopkins Bros., and Winton Lumber Co. In addition to lines in Idaho there were several logging lines across the mountains in Montana. The Hadley Mill, Mann Lumber Company, and the Montana Logging Company each had logging railroads along the St. Regis River.

All of these various railroads in the Coeur d'Alenes helped to open the area to development and settlement in a manner that would have been impossible otherwise. Today nearly all these lines are gone, but the prosperous, exciting days they once brought will not easily be forgotten.

Chapter Six

Fighting Snow

RAILROADING IN THE COEUR D'ALENES was not without its danger even during the height of summer — what with the threats of forest fires, runaway trains on the steep grades, labor violence, or a myriad of other possible ills; but undoubtedly the most trying challenge of all was the winter snow.

The snowfall in the Coeur d'Alenes was certainly prodigious, although some of the early reports might be questioned due to drifting, slides, or just plain exaggeration. While there were some claims in the 1890s of up to 15 feet of snow in the passes and more in canyons, not all claims were suspect. Even down in Wallace the total snowfall during the winter of 1889–1890 was said to be 17½ feet, and in the spring of 1892 NP superintendent Ramsey rode over Lookout Pass and reported ten feet of snow at the summit.

While the difficulties of the NP operating over Lookout Pass are easy to visualize, the less apparent winter obstacles for the OR&N were also considerable. The Palouse country around Tekoa with its open rolling hills just invited huge snowdrifts. A good example occurred in the early spring of 1890. A series of heavy snowstorms in the mining area failed to stop the OR&N, but when the wind started to blow on the Palouse snow blocked the line beyond Tekoa for a whole week, and even after the line was cleared for a few days it drifted shut again.

Many of the stories about winter railroading in the Coeur d'Alenes involve the terror of disasters or near disasters at the hand of nature, but though the railroad men might approach these dangers with apprehension, there was a certain sense of awe, fascination, and beauty in this season as well. There were even occasions of hilarity amid the perils which helped to make them bearable.

The earliest attempts of these railroads to handle this winter snowfall are mostly lost in the past, but as the CR&N certainly didn't have a rotary snowplow on the narrow gauge it is reasonable to assume they did use some type of wedge plow. This could have been mounted on the front of an engine, or might have ridden on its own set of wheels. Unfortunately available photographs fail to show any plows on that line.

Records do indiate that CR&N engines were used to "buck" the snow — presumably with a wedge plow. (Bucking snow was an extremely dangerous operation in which the locomotive with the plow would run at speed into the drifts of snow and continue until it stalled. Then it would back a respectable distance and run at the obstacle again. The dangers of this operation were many, for the engine could easily be derailed and overturn. This danger

This tremendous snowslide of February 3, 1890, blocked the CR&N narrow gauge in Canyon Creek. At the end of the month, after the railroad was reopened, the *Wallace Free Press* described the trip to Burke as "through solid palisades of snow."

was compounded when more than one locomotive was used, for the combined units frequently "jackknifed" together.)

On one occasion in the spring of 1890, three CR&N engines (practically the whole roster) bucked their way through an extremely heavy snowfall to Burke! But in another two weeks Canyon Creek had become impassable. The "Big 4" tried to buck past the Frisco Mine and failed. It was reported that 55 feet of snow (apparently from slides) covered the track in one place.

While no serious mishaps are known to have resulted from bucking on the CR&N, the dangers of this practice did not fail to completely bypass this line. In the spring of 1891 the "Big Four" was "jammed up" while bucking snow and was out of commission for over two weeks. Luckily there were no human casualties.

Although wedge plows could be used in light snowfalls, a primary method of deep snow removal (even with the coming of the standard gauge rotary plows) was back-breaking hand shoveling. On the occasion mentioned in the spring of 1890, the narrow gauge had over 100 men digging on Canyon Creek. This hand work was not only difficult, but extremely dangerous. The 1890 slides on Canyon Creek claimed the lives of four shovelers, and a slide at the head of Nine Mile Canyon killed another six men at the Custer Mine.

The coming of the standard gauge NP and OR&N lines did bring the awesome steam-powered rotary snowplows which did take some of the burden off the hand shovelers. These plows were vastly superior to wedge plows as their spinning blade could safely operate in much deeper snow; nevertheless, even these plows had limitations that were soon pointed out.

As mentioned in Chapter Four, the newly completed Coeur d'Alene Branch of the NP was blocked by snow throughout its first winter of 1890–1891, and the *Wallace Press* quickly suggested the following on January 2, 1891:

The Northern Pacific should lose no time in tunneling the Mullan pass [Lookout Pass]. Snow plows and rotary shovels are all right on a level plain and a moderate grade, but on such a rise and descent as that of the Mullan divide the snow falls too deep to be put out of the way. This seems to have been demonstrated already with only a five foot fall of snow. What will be the result later on with about a twenty-one foot fall!

While there is no doubt that the rotaries were destined to have a great struggle keeping Lookout Pass open, the predicted 21-foot snowfall didn't materialize. Actually the biggest problem for the rotary was not the depth of the snowfall itself, but the slides it might produce. As a snowslide generally carried rocks and trees across the track, it was not prudent to push the spinning blade of the rotary into the mass of a slide containing such hidden obstacles. In this case it was necessary for men to precede the rotary and probe for hidden debris. If the slide was too deep, or debris was found, hand shovelers had to dig into the snow and remove it. The "clean" snow was then shoveled back to the blade of the rotary and thrown out of the cut.

One of the worst series of snowslides took place early in 1894. Both Lookout Pass and Canyon Creek were to suffer huge slides and in the end five men would die. T. N. Barnard photographed the aftermath of the slides and the *Coeur d'Alene Miner* gave a first-hand account, so today we can get some idea of the extent and power of these "white mountains." The first slides took place just above the "S" bridge as the *Coeur d'Alene Miner* related on January 20, 1894.

Barnard-Stockbridge Collection
University of Idaho Library
NP plow train working on the slide of January 20, 1894, just above the "S" bridge (upper right).

Barnard-Stockbridge Collection
University of Idaho Library
Looking upgrade at the January 20, 1894 slide just above the "S" bridge. The small trestle on the left is where the line recrosses Willow Creek forming the loop.

The snowslide on the NP which came down a week ago Thursday a few miles east of Mullan, is still blockading the road, but it is expected the line will be open for traffic by tomorrow night. A force of over thirty men has been constantly employed since the slide occurred. The slide covered the track for a distance of about 500 feet and in some places to a depth of thirty feet. The snow is packed almost as solid as ice and is thoroughly mixed with boulders and logs, so that the removal is exceedingly difficult. There is a deep cut for almost the whole distance which adds immensely to the work of removing the snow and debris. The logs and boulders have to be dragged out and the snow, after being loosened, is thrown out by the rotary snowplow. There have been several other smaller slides in the mean time, but they are insignificant compared with the one in question. T. N. Barnard, the photographer of this city, took a photograph of the slide Monday.

These slides were finally cleared and the line opened to Missoula on February first. But this was only the start of the troubles. Later in February the *Coeur d'Alene Miner* (February 24, 1894) related the story of an accident in Canyon Creek that could easily have been deadly, but was told in an outright facetious manner.

Last Sunday morning the rotary plow on the Northern Pacific jumped the track at Gem and took out the entire porch in front of White & Bender's store, plowing into the frozen ground to a depth of three feet. The sudden leap was caused by coming at once in contact with a layer of snow which had been trampled solid by pedestrians. The water pipes were torn up and a general wreck made of everything in reach of the iron jaws of the ponderous machine.

The rotary was dragged from its lair in front of White & Bender's store at Gem on Thursday afternoon. Strange to say, it had suffered no material damage, although one or two iron braces were bent while the great track cleaner was engaged in chewing up White & Bender's porch.

Not content with embarrassing the railroad with this story, the editor added insult to injury by running the following story about the rotary's engineer in another part of the same paper.

The ditching of the rotary snowplow at Gem

last Sunday made it necessary for the train men to remain there until the plow was replaced on the track. Engineer Snyder, of the wrecked rotary, evidently had this in mind when he struck Mrs. Murphy for a rate of three meals for $1. Supposing his salary to be not more than $1.50 per day, the generous landlady acquiesced. Snyder had not passed out of sight when Engineer Cheeny, who drives the big "hog" behind the rotary, came up to pay for his ample meal. Mrs. Murphy knew him and taxed him four bits, "But that poor fellow," she said pointing to Snyder, "He can't afford to pay that much, so I give him three meals for $1." The boys say she took Snyder for a "Jerry" [common laborer] instead of a four-dollar a day man with over time.

Unfortunately it was not possible for all the stories that year of 1894 to be lighthearted. The heavy accumulation of snow that winter was poised high on the steep slopes of Canyon Creek and sudden warming and rain were all that waited to set disaster in motion. These elements came together on March 29, 1894. The result was five people killed and tremendous destruction. Fortunately most of the slides were away from the towns this time. Again Barnard photographs and the *Miner* articles graphically show the tremendous power of these slides. The following *Coeur d'Alene Miner* article was published on April 7, 1894.

The slides in Canyon Creek have continued all week to attract a considerable number of visitors to see these disastrous and awful manifestations of the forces of nature. The Northern Pacific now takes passengers and freight up as far as the second slide. This is not more than two and one-half miles from Burke, whence passengers travel afoot, and the freight is dragged over the slides on sleds and afterwards hauled up to Burke on push cars, making three portages over the slides. The railroad track is absolutely clear of snow, except at the points covered with slides, necessitating several changes from sled to push cart and vice versa.

At the Black Bear slide the Northern suffered but little compared with the Union Pacific. The latter has had a large force of men and a rotary at work there since Monday but has not yet cut

Two rotary snowplows attacking one of the slides of March 29, 1894, near Black Bear on Canyon Creek. This view looking down canyon shows the NP plow on the right and the OR&N plow on the left.

The NP rotary working on another slide near Mace on May 1, 1894. The slide at this point was said to be 86 feet deep!

through. At the second slide, about three-fourths of a mile further up the canyon, both railroad companies had a number of laborers — the Union about 80 and the Northern about 40, until the strike which occurred Thursday noon. [The snow shovelers went on strike for $2 a day. Their previous wages were between $1.50 and $1.65 a day.] Therefore the Union has made more headway at this point than the Northern. Here the Northern blasted out the face of the cut with dynamite and then threw out the snow with the rotary, first picking out the logs and boulders, while the Union depended entirely on shoveling the snow out by succesive stages. The snow here, contains comparatively few logs or boulders, as is the case with the third slide, which is only 300 to 400 feet above the second. These cover the railroads to a depth of 40 feet, and each one is several hundred feet in length, presenting a complete barrier from wall to wall of the canyon. High upon the slope of the mountain fully half a mile distant may be seen the line where they began. The snow converged to the respective gulches and gathering speed and volume at every leap, dashed downward like a cataract expending its tremendous energy upon the base of the opposing mountain.

Half a mile further up is the fourth slide, this involves both railroad tracks for a length of several thousand feet, but differs from those already seen in that it is filled with green timber, twisted into every conceivable shape. This ran through a grove of saplings six to nine inches in diameter, breaking off some and tearing up others by the roots. The snow is green with the foliage of the pines, and about one-half of the mass appears to be logs and saplings.

This is the last slide affecting the Northern Pacific, but a few hundred feet above the Standard ore bin is another one that covers the Union Pacific track for 200 to 300 feet. This holds a considerable proportion of logs and boulders. At the last turn on the road to Burke there is still another one which came down on the fateful 29th of March, but this stopped just short of the Union Pacific railroad. All the slides were on the northern slope of the canyon where the snow had, of course, accumulated in much greater quantities than on the other side. This is the sixth slide between Gem and Burke. These magnificent and appalling specimens of natures handiwork are well worthy of a trip of many miles to see them. There need not be any hurry, however, as they may still be seen to advantage after the railroads are in operation. There will be snow there nearly all summer.

The summer was nearly gone when

the tracks were cleared to Burke. The NP resumed its operations on July thirty-first, and began to haul 12 to 15 carloads of ore out each day in an effort to catch up on the backlog waiting shipment. Although the snow had begun to melt away, it would be a long time before the fear of slides would fade from the minds of Canyon Creek residents. But time did have a way of easing fears, and it was not until 1910 that fatal slides struck again with even more fury. The intervening years occasioned what was perhaps the most spectacular nonfatal railroad accident not just in this area, but perhaps in the whole country.

The following account of the great "S" bridge wreck was published on February 11, 1903, in the *Idaho State Tribune*. This version of the story was

Barnard-Stockbridge Collection
University of Idaho Library
Hand digging on the 1894 slides near Mace, probably on the OR&N line.

also carried on the back of Barnard Studio's views of the disaster.

Shortly after 7 o'clock yesterday morning there occurred on the NP RR at the "S" bridge above Mullan what might have been under other circumstances one of the most serious railroad catastrophes which ever happened in the Northwest. The fact of a locomotive plunging over 80 feet through a bridge followed by a caboose containing eight men and no one killed will be considered nothing short of a miracle. It was one of those particular cases where 30 feet of snow answered the purpose of a life perserver.

The great rotary snowplow of the NP road, operating between Wallace and Saltese over the Bitter Root mountains was at the head of the train and was moved by engine No. 68 with Engineer George Morse at the throttle. Behind the snow plow was a helping engine [actually this was engine No. 68 which was just mentioned] and behind that was the passenger train with engine 398 [the correct number was 396]. Engineer Tyner, Fireman Leslie Adams and Conductor George Reimer in charge. Behind the passenger was a caboose and behind that was a 12-wheeled [actually a 2-8-0] hog engine No. 79,

Barnard-Stockbridge Collection
University of Idaho Library

NP engine No. 79 and the caboose which fell about 80 feet from the "S" bridge without loss of a single life.

Barnard-Stockbridge Collection
University of Idaho Library

The "S" bridge wreck of February 10, 1903. The NP rotary is followed by engines No. 68 and No. 396.

with Engineer Philips and Fireman Saterston in charge. All these sections were coupled together and were stalled in the snow near Dorsey and were attempting to work their way back to Wallace, the rotary plow having broken down. The various train crews had worked until 4:10 in the morning with very little success and at times had some wheels off the track. Section by section were shoveled out and they had succeeded in getting the trains back as far as the "S" bridge. Engine 79, the caboose and the rear end of the passenger coach stood on the bridge. Several members of the engine and train crews being almost exhausted from overwork, went into the caboose to sleep. They entered it

Coeur d'Alene District Mining Museum
An NP rotary at work near the Snowstorm
Mine above Mullan.

shortly after 4 o'clock and all the trains coupled together stood there until shortly after 7 o'clock when a snow slide reaching far up the mountain came tearing down the narrow gorge carrying away the foundation of the upper trestles of the upper end of the "S" bridge on which stood the engine, caboose and rear passenger coach. The engine and caboose plunged into the chasm below. The fall was 80 feet. The engine buried itself completely out of sight in 30 feet of snow. The caboose shot down endwise and like an arrow plunged into the snowbank at the bottom, carrying with it its eight occupants. Fortunately there were no persons on the engine at the time it made the awful plunge. In the caboose were Engineer Philips, Fireman Staterston, Breakman [*sic*] Grant, Conductor Smith, Breakman [*sic*] Maxwell, Fireman Rice, Breakman [*sic*] Merritt and a section hand from Mullan whose name we did not learn. In the passenger coach there were eight or nine passengers and as the engine and caboose went down the passenger coach hung over the break in the bridge and stood on an angle of 45 degrees, but was prevented from falling by the coupling to the coach ahead. Among the passengers was Jack Daly, one of the good natured business men of Saltese, and he seems to have furnished the clown side to this narrow escape from serious injury if not instant death. When the bridge gave way and the coach slid down to its angular position the glass in the windows were broken. Daly jumped through a window, fell eighty feet, lighted in the great gorge of snow below, pulled himself out, climbed up the mountain side, went into the coach, put on his shoes and spent the balance of the time shaking hands with himself and expressing his thanks for his narrow escape. The other passengers in the coach clung to the side and drew themselves to the front end and quietly passed into the next coach, which did not happen to be far enough over the bridge to be caught in the break. Charles Smith the conductor, was unconscious for two hours but when revived was able to care for himself without much assistance.

The "S" bridge where this accident happened is so called because it is constructed in the form of letter "S" and is 300 feet long, is very high and spans Willow Creek. It was built in serpentine shape for the reason that it is at a point where the road makes a short loop in the mountain climb over the Bitter Root summit. The tracks after this loop is made over the "S" bridge come very nearly together, the one several feet above the other, but at most they are only sixty feet apart. At the time of the construction of this bridge it was considered a wonderful success in

Beautiful 1898 view of NP plow No. 6 and 2-8-0 No. 97 somewhere on the Coeur d'Alene Branch, possibly at Mullan.

railroad engineering. The snowslide yesterday which carried down the engine and caboose [also carried] away nine bents of this wonderful structure.

Although the "S" bridge wreck of 1903 had all the makings of a great disaster that failed to materialize, the real thing was not long in coming. Earlier snowslides in Canyon Creek Canyon had shown the potential for tremendous loss of life, but so far had avoided the more densely populated areas. In the spring of 1910 time ran out for the town of Mace. On February tenth at 11:00 P.M. a great wall of snow thundered down on the houses of that town leaving 19 persons dead in its wake. The next morning at 3:00 A.M. another slide hit Burke killing five for a total of 24 dead. This was the greatest loss of life from snow in the history of the Coeur d'Alenes. Again, as in 1894, the tracks of both the NP and OR&N were blocked by the slides, and weeks passed before they were cleared. While these were not the last lives lost to slides in this canyon, residents there gained a respect for

Plowing on the east side of the pass in the late afternoon. Note the long shadows of winter on the snow.

An early NP plow train headed downgrade across the "S" bridge.

Coeur d'Alene District Mining Museum

Two rotaries meeting east of Lookout. The location may be Sohon Spur.

possible slide areas and the future tolls from them were much lower.

Snowslides also continued to be a problem on Lookout Pass. In the spring of 1916 a slide destroyed much of the great trestle at Dorsey, and by the time it was repaired two weeks later the line had drifted in solid. This occasioned two snowplow trains, one working from Wallace east — the other from St. Regis west, and resulted in some of the most spectacular snowplow photographs ever taken. The train originating in Wallace was composed of NP's No. 6 rotary and *four* locomotives! The first engine is unidentifiable (probably a 2-8-0), the second was No. 1319 (a 4-6-0), the third No. 1310 (another 4-6-0), and the last engine is believed to be No. 74 (a 2-8-0). The

Barnard-Stockbridge Collection
University of Idaho Library

Earlier view of a rotary at Saltese — this one in 1894. The plow, built by Alco (Cooke) appears to be one constructed for the OR&N and it is unclear how it came to be used on the NP.

Standow Photo
Barnard-Stockbridge Collection
University of Idaho Library
Aftermath of the terrible snowslide at Mace on February 10, 1910, which killed 19 people. The smoke at the bottom is from an NP engine and the locomotive on the right is OR&N No. 163.

train from St. Regis had No. 1217 (a 2-8-0) and No. 1223 (another 2-8-0). This last engine ran in reverse so it could better help the train to back if the rotary became stalled. The two trains met just west of the pass, the train from St. Regis having covered the largest portion of the route when the Wallace train apparently encountered much heavier drifts.

The slide that had taken out the Dorsey trestle, like that causing the great "S" bridge wreck, had not claimed any lives, but this good fortune eventually ran out. On February 29, 1936, NP passenger train No. 255 headed by engine No. 1387 (a 4-6-0) was hit by a tremendous snowslide just east of Lookout (at a point between Borax and Sohon). Conductor Byall, brakeman Brill, and one passenger were killed. It is interesting that passenger service had operated over Lookout for years without one passenger fatality, and then when only a few years of passenger service remained, the record was broken.

Changes in the method of snow removal eventually came just as changes in service had come. Diesel locomotives replaced steam locomotives, but the steam-powered rotaries lasted a little longer. In the end bulldozers replaced the great rotaries. Bulldozers could be

R. V. Nixon Collection
The trestle at Dorsey was taken out by a snowslide in the spring of 1916. Two weeks passed before the damage could be repaired. Here engine No. 3101, a 2-6-6-2, heads a work train engaged in the rebuilding.

Ralph Cuplin Photo
W. R. McGee Collection
The westbound plow near the Borax Tunnel with engine No. 1217 pushing. Behind it, out of the picture, was another engine, No. 1223, running in reverse.

Ralph Cuplin Photo
W. R. McGee Collection

Westbound plow train at the summit showing engine No. 1223 running in reverse.

Ralph Cuplin Photo
R. V. Nixon Collection

Now above the Borax Tunnel the train continues on toward Lookout Pass.

hauled in by flatcar and dropped off at trouble spots. Rather than plow a channel through the snow which increased the problem of drifting, the bulldozers could leave the rails and push the snow over the edge of the hill. Also this ability to leave the rails made it possible for trains to pass where they were working and speeded operations.

While the new method of snow removal may have been more efficient, there is no doubt that the rotary's great spinning wheel throwing its white

Ralph Cuplin Photo
Coeur d'Alene District Mining Museum

The east bound snowplow train resting on the newly repaired Dorsey Trestle. The train was composed of rotary No. 6, an unidentified 4-6-0, engine No. 1319 (a 4-6-0), engine No. 1310 (another 4-6-0), and an unidentified 2-8-0.

Ralph Cuplin Photo
W. R. McGee Collection

At last! The two plow trains meet just west of Lookout Pass and the blockade of the Coeur d'Alene branch is over. The westbound train is on the right and the eastbound on the left.

R. V. Nixon Photo
This snowslide on February 29, 1936, occurred just east of Lookout Pass. Three people were killed as a result; conductor Byall, brakeman Brill, and one passenger.

Ralph Cuplin Photo
Coeur d'Alene District Mining Museum
Plowing on the four percent grade above Dorsey created this spectacular scene of winter railroading in the Coeur d'Alenes.

plume of snow far to the side, and sending a dark column of smoke high in the air, was a spectacle that could hardly be matched by a bulldozer! But now the line over Lookout has been abandoned and even the sound of the bulldozer working to clear the tracks is gone. The deep blanket of white the railroad fought for 89 years is now the master again.

Dr. Philip R. Hastings Photo
Z-3 2-8-8-2 No. 4020 enveloped by steam as it heaved to a stop at the summit of Lookout Pass, so the crew could set up retainers for the trip down the other side. February 24, 1951.

Extra 4020 East starts gingerly down the four percent grade of the east slope of Lookout Pass, headed for St. Regis, Montana, with a few gondola loads of ore concentrate February 24, 1951.

Z-3 2-8-8-2 No. 4020 was dwarfed by the Bitter Root Mountains as it coasted down the east slope of Lookout Pass with the daily freight from Wallace, Idaho, to St. Regis, Montana. The location is Copper Gulch, Montana, on February 24, 1951.

Chapter Seven

Other Wrecks and Disasters

ALTHOUGH SNOW RELATED ACCIDENTS accounted for a large number of the accidents that occurred in the Coeur d'Alenes, other causes certainly existed. Fire, flood, mechanical failures, human error, and human violence also caused much destruction and loss of life.

The old CR&N was very unusual as it had a perfect record of zero facilities re-lated to service throughout its entire history (notwithstanding a couple of workers killed in construction and the snow shovelers mentioned in the previous chapter), unlike both the OR&N and NP which had fatalities early after their arrival in this area. This good record was largely due to the low speed at which the narrow gauge trains generally oper-

Eastern Washington State Historical Society

This derailment of OR&N No. 72 took place at Lacon, Idaho (just west of Harrison on Coeur d'Alene Lake), on July 4, 1906. Train No. 11 was headed westbound toward Spokane led by 4-4-0 No. 72 when the engine hit a section of washed-out track. Engineer Perley and the fireman were slightly scalded. The conductor of the ill-fated train was Bob Jewell. This view shows the timbers used to block up the engine and the ropes that righted it.

Eastern Washington State Historical Society

This interesting wrecker and OR&N engine No. 147, a 4-6-0, were used to rescue engine No. 72.

Eastern Washington State Historical Society

Here the men are working to replace the lead truck (one wheel of this is visible on the extreme left) under the front of the engine. In the foreground can be seen the rope block and tackle used and the inevitable group of small children that flocked to such events. In the background is Coeur d'Alene Lake.

ated, for this line was certainly not without accidents. Derailments were a common occurrence on the line and their threat was an extremely serious one. In addition to the possibility of being crushed, those in the cab of a locomotive during a derailment were exposed to the additional danger of being scalded by live steam. This danger to the crew made it advisable for them to jump from the locomotive when a wreck was eminent, and resulted in the following story about the CR&N which appeared in the *Wallace Free Press* of February 15, 1890.

A Locomotive Fireman's Jump

While the passenger train was coming down Kingston hill Thursday afternoon the engine [No. 3] struck a small rock slide. The slide being on a curve the engineer did not see the pile of rocks until too close to stop. Engineer Manchester whistled for brakes and reversed the lever, and then Manchester and fireman Brewer jumped. The train stopped with a slight jar and no damage was done. Fireman Brewer is now the champion jumper of the Coeur d'Alene, as his leap by actual measurement is nearly fifty feet. [This is just as it was reported!] If the train had left the track it would have been a serious accident, for the cars would have rolled down the hill to the creek 50 feet or more. The train was delayed an hour and a half. Conductor Brown is a handy man with a shovel, for he made the earth and rocks fly from the track like a rotary snowplow would the white element.

In this case the "unnecessary" jump makes fireman Brewer appear rather cowardly, but this was hardly the case. Brewer's prudence was established three months later on May first when the same engine plunged into the river near Kingston. On this occasion Brewer, now as engineer, and Owen McClure, fireman, saved their lives only by jumping from the cab.

Many of the derailments in the spring of 1890 were due to the heavy snow the previous winter, for inevitably this brought severe flooding and landslides

A landslide caused this derailment of NP No. 22 on November 22, 1904. The location was two miles west of Iron Mountain, Montana (across the Clark Fork River from Superior).

as the weather warmed. In 1890 the flooding caused washouts for both the narrow gauge and the OR&N.

Three days before the CR&N No. 3 went in the river at Kingston the OR&N suffered a similar accident. Water undermined the grade a mile and a half above Wallace and the track collapsed

If you have ever wondered what would have happened if a train derailed while crossing an old-style wooden truss bridge, here is the answer. Note the iron rods wrapped around the wreckage. On January 31, 1906, NP engines 381 and 1310 jumped the track while crossing the St. Regis River on bridge No. 17 east of Haugan, Montana. Killed in the accident were fireman Burse and conductor McDonald.

under engine No. 26 causing it and the tender to fall down a six-foot embankment into the river. The engineer, Denny Sheehy, was cut about the head and just escaped before the water caught him in the cab, while the fireman, Tim O'Leary, didn't receive a scratch.

Washouts due to flooding were a continuing problem in the Coeur d'Alenes, especially in the years 1890 (as just mentioned), 1893, 1894, and 1896. The spring of 1894 was particularly disasterous. In May water was reportedly two feet above the tracks at Harrison, and between Cataldo and Kingston the

CR&N narrow guage engine No. 1 in the Coeur d'Alene River ca. 1889. However, the date could be a little later as the engine has been relettered for the NP on the cab. Unfortunately the details of this accident have been lost in the past.

Flooding in the spring of 1894 was a foretaste of what was to come in 1933. The heavy winter snows melted too suddenly and the resulting flooding of the St. Regis River on the Montana side of the divide was so bad that the NP line was not in regular operation until late July. This shoo-fly track was between Saltese and St. Regis.

These runaway OR&N ballast cars (used as ore cars) derailed on the high-line leading to the Mammoth and Standard (later Federal Mining & Smelting) mills on Canyon Creek. The switch to this line was often thrown to stop runaways as it diverted them up a steep grade. This trestle crossing Canyon Creek is not far from the switch. Note the Fox trucks used on the cars.

This 1913 runaway of OWR&N 2-8-0 No. 325 and its ore cars on the Federal highline easily have claimed a number of lives, but the train happened to be unmanned. Somehow the train got away when the crew was not aboard, and it continued to gain speed down the steep Canyon Creek grade until sent up the highline where it derailed. Here, near the switch, several ore cars and the tender of No. 325 left the rails. Barely in the picture on the left is the rescue train with a wrecking crane. Just out of the picture to the right is the trestle over Canyon Creek.

tracks were almost completely covered. Washouts were especially numerous on the OR&N track with damage so bad between Wallace and Mullan that that track was abandoned the following year. The NP also had so much trouble on the line to Missoula that it was not in operation until late in July! But these early floods were only a foretaste of the great flood of 1933 which will be covered later in this chapter.

In addition to derailments and washouts, the steep grades of Canyon Creek Canyon and Lookout Pass made runaway cars and locomotives an extremely serious danger right from the earliest days. Luckily it was rare for a locomotive to runaway, but there were a number of runaway cars — on the average of several a year.

In June of 1891 the OR&N had a car runaway in Mullan, race through Wallace, and finally stop when it reached a nearly level stretch at Kingston. The av-

Barnard-Stockbridge Collection
University of Idaho Library

The weight of engine No. 325 carried it further up the high-line and off the trestle into Canyon Creek. The cab of the engine was pointing up the high-line to the right as it had runaway in reverse. As there was no way to turn an engine in the canyon, they always ran pointed upstream (to the left in this picture).

erage speed of the car was estimated to be in excess of 70 m.p.h.! It was amazing that no one was injured, but even more so that the car stayed on the track.

Two months later the CR&N had a narrow gauge handcar get away at Burke and the *Wallace Press* of August 1, 1891, reported that two miles down canyon it ran into locomotive No. 1 "smashing the headlight, number plate and some other small portions of its anatomy and giving the train crew that glorious railroad man's privilege, a chance for an all round kick [gripe]."

The next day a serious runaway killed brakeman Michael Mullan when two OR&N boxcars loaded with concentrates got away at the Gem Mine. The brakeman rode the top of the car until it derailed at the wye just above Wallace throwing him to his death.

R.V. Nixon Collection

On January 16, 1930, NP engine No. 3015 (a 2-6-6-2) ran away on the four percent grade east of Lookout. The engine and its train left the track on the first big curve about two miles from the summit. The wreck, said to be caused by a frozen air line, killed engineer Campbell and brakeman Erickson. Fireman Swant was badly injured and scalded but managed to get out of the wreckage and walked back to Lookout. The engine was dismantled on the spot and hauled away in pieces.

Barnard-Stockbridge Collection
University of Idaho Library

Runaway cars down Nine Mile Canyon resulted in this wreck beside the NP depot in Wallace. Particulars of this accident have been lost, so it is not known if there were any casualites. The date was about 1910. Note the freight house (old narrow gauge depot) on this end of the station and the "NP House" hotel across the street.

Barnard-Stockbridge Collection
University of Idaho Library

The boiler explosion of NP No. 79 at Mace on December 6, 1907, graphically illustrated the importance of keeping adequate water in the boiler. No. 79, a 2-8-0, was headed up canyon when the explosion disintegrated the engine. Looking down canyon behind the tender, one can see the Mace schoolhouse, and to the left is the OR&N track.

This fatality was not the first related to rail service, for little more than a month earlier that distinction had already been claimed in another OR&N accident. On June 20, 1891, the *Wallace Press* related:

R. V. Nixon Collection

Here are the remains of No. 79 being inspected by several men. The location is believed to be down the canyon at Wallace.

"First fatal railroad accident in Coeur d'Alenes known to a railroad train service man took place last Saturday afternoon at 2:45. Joe Clark lost life."

The regular Union Pacific passenger pulled in McMahon's circus advance car, which was fitted with the old-fashioned Miller couplings. It became necessary to attach the same to a refrigerator car standing on a curved sidetrack, just back of the depot. Brakeman Clark undertook to make the coupling, and owing to the curve in the track the patent coupling slipped past the other car bumper and rolled Mr. Clark out from between the dead woods on the cars. He fell on the rails. He died several hours later of internal bleeding.

A similar accident took place last November on the "little road" [CR&N] but Wm. Donnelly stood on the outside of the curve and the accident was not serious.

Mismatched couplers which resulted in this death were a common danger throughout the country in this day when many new designs were being tried.

The Coeur d'Alenes also saw another type of accident that was all too common nationally, the so-called "cornfield meet" (collision of two trains). Luckily the few occasions these occurred in the area they were rather minor. The following account in the *Wallace Press* (April 11, 1891) even takes a light-hearted view of what could have been a very serious affair.

Two Union Pacific engines which could not pass each other on the same track "telescoped" at the point just below the NP depot last Saturday morning. The shock did considerable damage to the combatants, but fortunately no lives were lost, although some ladies from Osburn, among whom was Richard Wilson, were terribly frightened. It seems that the collision was a pure accident. The switch engine was going down to the yards from the depot and met the up-coming freight.

It should be noted that while Richard Wilson objected to the implication that he was frightened along with the ladies, the editor of the *Press* took all the more delight in satirizing him. Since there was little legal recourse, papers of this day often carried personal attacks. This certainly "spiced up" the material, but woe be to the person that got on the wrong side of the editor.

Returning to the subject at hand, we come in 1899 to the unfortunate story of the destruction of the Bunker Hill con-

R. V. Nixon Collection

Cornfield meets were rare in the Coeur d'Alenes, but there are records of several. This collision occurred between Wallace and Mullan about 1916. The Mullan local passenger train headed by NP 2-8-0 No. 93 was struck by engine No. 1216, another 2-8-0 which was running in reverse to Wallace after operating as a helper up Lookout Pass. Apparently No. 1216 misread its orders to wait on a siding for the passenger train to pass.

centrator, the cause of which was deliberate and not accidental. Labor unrest earlier in July of 1892 had resulted in the dynamiting of the Frisco mill. Troops were called in and an uneasy peace returned.

In 1899 this peace was broken when union miners again resorted to violence,

Hutton Collection
Eastern Washington State Historical Society

This engine, NP 2-8-0 No. 485, was reportedly the one hijacked on April 29, 1899, and used to carry the men and dynamite which destroyed the Bunker Hill Mill. Engineer Levi Hutton and his wife appear before the engine and the two-stall engine house in Wallace.

this time against the Bunker Hill and Sullivan which steadfastly continued to employ nonunion workers. The union wanted a uniform wage of $3.50 a day for miners, car men, and shovelers, but the Bunker Hill refused setting off a strike on April twenty-sixth. The attack came on the twenty-ninth when several hundred armed men commandeered the NP local at Burke. Four masked men climbed in the cab with engineer Al Hutton and ordered him to take them to Wardner. At Gem they took 3,000 pounds of dynamite from the powder

magazine of the Helena-Frisco Mine and loaded it on the train. Additional men also joined the train as it proceeded down the canyon.

At Wallace it was necessary for the NP train to switch over to OR&N track for the remainder of the trip as the NP had no standard gauge line to Wardner. Since the NP train had no rights on the OR&N track, Hutton warned the masked men of a possible "cornfield meet," but continued when ordered — with a frequent blowing of his whistle.

When the train arrived at Wardner

Barnard-Stockbridge Collection
University of Idaho Library

The remains of the Bunker Hill Mill after the great blast. OR&N engine No. 113 is apparently being put to use during the clean up.

about 11:00 A.M., the Bunker Hill had already been warned of the approaching danger. The crowd on the train, now estimated at 1,000 men alighted and headed for the saloons in a festive mood. The 60 to 70 boxes of dynamite were unloaded by some of the men who remained. When the others returned from drinking and started to advance toward the Bunker Hill and Sullivan concentrator, Sheriff James Young tried to talk them out of it, but to no avail. A few Bunker Hill employees fired at the crowd as it approached but soon ran for cover. The explosives were planted and the resulting blast obliterated the concentrator, compressor, electric plant, and boardinghouse — to cheers of the union men. The group then boarded the train and returned to Wallace and Burke.

This time 500 troops were sent to the Coeur d'Alenes and martial law was declared again. In the aftermath the sheriff was impeached for failing to stop the miners; and Hutton, the engineer, was imprisoned for a time under the belief he had deliberately helped the union men. The bad feelings generated between the union and management continued to drag on for years.

The next great disaster to hit the Coeur d'Alenes was due to natural rather than human causes. This disaster, the great 1910 forest fire, or "Big Blowup" left at least 85 dead and caused several hundred million dollars in damage. Forest fires had always been a problem in the area, but up to this time they had burned themselves out before seriously endangering any populated areas.

The year of 1910 had begun with the snowslide disaster at Mace (related in Chapter Seven), and as summer came

the heat rose and the humidity dropped. With the ensuing drought came numerous forest fires. In District One of the Forest Service, a 64 square mile area of which the Coeur d'Alenes were a part, about 3,000 fires were burning. Fire fighting in the forests was in its infancy and there was not much crews could do with a really serious fire; nevertheless, approximately 3,000 men were at work in the district — an average of one per fire!

If luck had prevailed as in the past, the fires would have remained mostly separate and would have burned themselves out as the rains of fall began. But this was not to be. On August twentieth wind struck from the southwest and soon reached hurricane level. Numerous small fires were blown together as some traveled at the speed of 70 m.p.h., and the resulting conflagration began to create its own weather system, much like the "fire-storms" that were caused by bombing in Europe during World War II. In Denver the temperature dropped 19 degrees in ten minutes and a 42 m.p.h. wind hit as the "Big Blow" pulled in more oxygen to feed itself.

The town of Wallace was threatened as flames approached from the southwest. Five rescue trains were made up by the NP and OR&N. Hundreds of women, children, and men unable to fight fire crowded into the odd assortment of coaches, baggage cars and boxcars that made up the consists. After waiting for several hours, perhaps to assure that no one was forgotten, the trains left with their now frantic passengers.

The OR&N carried refugees west with some stopping at Harrison or Coeur d'Alene, and others continuing to Spokane. The NP carried its precious cargo eastward to Missoula through the perilous fires which were often burning on either side of the track. NP engineers McCann and Beebe reportedly piloted two of these trains.

The most exciting story concerned a last minute rescue effort that was apparently unplanned. The Providence Hospital at the eastern end of Wallace became threatened by the fire and evacuation of the patients to town became impossible. Dr. Quigley spied an NP engine and caboose standing at the Federal concentrators (originally Standard and Mammoth) just up Canyon Creek. He asked conductor George W. Brown for help, and the train was brought down to the hospital. Forty patients and 15 sisters were loaded into the caboose, in the tender, and even in the engine cab (one account also says there was a boxcar). Along with conductor Brown were engineer S. G. Whiting, fireman S. J. Viggo, and brakeman Mike Nicholson. With fire burning on both sides of the track the train set out for Missoula at 9:30 P.M.

For several days the only report on the train was that it had left Mullan and the NP believed it might be lost. Finally word arrived that it had reached Missoula late in the morning of the twenty-first.

The journey had been a nightmare of smoke, heat, and flame. As the train approached the "S" bridge it was already burning but engineer Whiting raced across reaching the other side with the caboose smoking. This was not the last of the terrors for the Dorsey trestle was also burning and there was fire at both ends of the Borax tunnel.

When they miraculously reached Saltese cars were added and engineer F. L. Senfel relieved Whiting. With fires still threatening the train continued to Missoula arriving there late the next morning. Conductor Brown who couldn't see and brakeman Nicholson who was unable to talk were taken to the hospital while the town did all it could to aid the refugees.

This same morning of the twenty-first supervisor Koch of District One boarded a train at Missoula with the intention of traveling as far west as the fires would permit. Leaving at 10 A.M. they reached St. Regis that afternoon. There they transferred to an NP freight sent as a rescue train and ran to Deborgia where the flames stopped them. After taking on more survivors they started back down the line with the canyon filled with fire. Their doom appeared certain when a burning tree fell across the track trapping them between walls of flame. Koch and several other men jumped from the boxcar into the searing heat and moved the obstruction just in time. The train thus made it back to St. Regis without losing a life.

The worst of the fire lasted about 48 hours and slowed when the wind suddenly dropped and the humidity rose on August twenty-second. The next night light rain fell in most areas of District One with snow at higher elevations, and on August thirty-first heavy rains brought an end to the fire season.

The small towns of Taft, Deborgia, and Haugan were completely destroyed along with the eastern third of Wallace. In Wallace two died — John G. Boyd, a retired NP agent, suffocated and an unidentified young man burned to death. Over 100 buildings were destroyed including the UP depot, the Coeur d'Alene Hardware and Foundry, the Sunset Brewery and the *Wallace Times*. At the mouth of Canyon Creek the Providence Hospital and Federal concentrators were saved as was the town of Burke. Total damage to Wallace was estimated at one million dollars.

The great 1910 fire leveled the east side of Wallace including the just completed OR&N depot. However, the walls of the station did remain and it was soon rebuilt.

While the eastern part of Wallace was destroyed in the 1910 fire, much of the town did survive as this view shows. Note in the right foreground OR&N No. 242. This Brooks 2-8-0 was the ex-Snake River Valley No. 202. Its Belpaire boiler was characteristic of the Great Northern and very unusual for engines of the UP system.

Lower Burke was destroyed by fire July 13, 1923. The Hecla Mill and both the NP and OWR&N depots were among the casualties. Some claimed that sparks from a passing NP train caused the conflagration.

In addition to the loss of the UP depot, the NP's Dorsey trestle and "S" bridge had burned and much track was damaged. But within ten days the Coeur d'Alene Branch was again operating in a fashion. Trains from the east would run as far as Dorsey where passengers would walk across the canyon spanned by the damaged trestle. On the other side another train would pick them up and continue the trip downhill to the "S" bridge. This was bypassed by the original switchback allowing the remainder of the trip to Wallace to continue unbroken. In this way some traffic could move as the trestles were being repaired.

The toll of the fire was staggering — 85 men dead, 3,000,000 acres burned, and 8,000,000,000 board feet of good timber destroyed! While impossible to accurately determine, it has been estimated that the damage was over $200,000,000.

Unfortunately the "Big Blowup" was not the last major fire in the district, for on July 13, 1923, the town of Burke (which had escaped in 1910) was ravaged by another fire. This time the fire apparently started within the city, and before it had run its course it had completely destroyed the lower portion of Burke which included the NP and OWR&N depots as well as the surface works of the Hecla mine. The total damage was estimated at about one million dollars. Some believed the fire had been caused by sparks from an NP locomotive which had passed earlier; but although this company was sued, it could not be proven.

In the rebuilding that followed the UP constructed a large, new depot somewhat further up the canyon which was apparently used by the NP as well.

Of all disasters in the area, the one having the most far reaching effects on the railroads of the Coeur d'Alenes was the terrible 1933 flood. Spring flooding, as mentioned earlier in this chapter, had been an annual problem in the Coeur d'Alenes, but in December, 1933, a highly unusual situation developed. The mountains were covered with their

Barnard-Stockbridge Collection
University of Idaho Library

The great 1933 flood ravaging the east (upper) end of Wallace on December 23. At this point the waters of Canyon Creek (coming from the right) joined the South Fork (from the left) and flowed downstream past the buildings on the left. The track on the left belonged to the OWR&N and the two on the right the NP.

usual winter blanket of white when a
chinook (warm winter wind) struck the
Bitter Root Mountains combined with a
record rainfall. As the melting snow
joined with the rain filling the streams
and rivers to overflowing, the OWR&N
track from Wallace to Coeur d'Alene
Lake was almost completely washed
away as were the roads, thus isolating
Kellogg and Wallace. The Pine Creek
and Idaho Northern branches of the
OWR&N were so devastated that they
were never rebuilt. Tracks in Wallace
and up Canyon Creek (both OWR&N
and NP) were left in the same condition,
but they were rebuilt.

The NP also suffered much damage in
addition to its Canyon Creek trackage,
for the Nine Mile branch was so bad a
portion of it was abandoned the next
year. On the Montana side of the divide
the NP track along the St. Regis River
was not spared. This caused the NP to
negotiate an agreement with the Milwaukee to use 19 miles of their track between Haugan and St. Regis, Montana,
so the NP could abandon its track which
was damaged.

The damage from the 1933 flood was
spread throughout North Idaho and
Western Montana and cost over
$3,500,000. It also speeded the aban-
donment of much of the railroad
mileage in the Coeur d'Alenes.

With this decline the railroads suffered less from accidents and attacks of
nature due in part to improved methods
of railroad safety, flood control, and
forest fire fighting. And with the abandonment of the BN line over Lookout
Pass, perhaps the greatest hazard to railroad men in the Coeur d'Alenes has also
been removed.

Although not railroad related, the
Sunshine Mine disaster must be men-

Tabor Photo
Barnard-Stockbridge Collection
University of Idaho Library

One mile below Wallace looking upstream toward
town revealed this damage to the OWR&N track. The
rest of the line clear to Coeur d'Alene Lake was in
about the same condition.

tioned due to the terrible loss of life that
resulted. The Sunshine Mine (the
world's largest silver mine) is located on
Big Creek between Kellogg and Osburn.
On May 2, 1972 fire broke out in the
mine and 91 miners lost their lives. Not
only was this the greatest loss of life in
the Coeur d'Alenes, but it was the worst
mining disaster in the country since
1917. Today a twice life size statue of a
miner stands by Interstate 90 near the
mine as a memorial to those men.

Barnard-Stockbridge Collection
University of Idaho Library

The 1933 flood waters from Nine Mile Creek washed
past the NP depot taking out the roadbed of the NP
and OWR&N tracks before emptying into the South
Fork just out of the picture in the foreground.

Chapter Eight

The Final Chapter

IN THE YEARS FOLLOWING THE 1933 flood (mentioned in the previous chapter) and with the subsequent abandonments which followed it, both the OWR&N and the NP continued to cut back both mileage and passenger service.

The UP (which leased the OWR&N in 1936) reduced the length of its Sierra Nevada Branch in 1941 and again in 1953 resulting in its current two-mile length. Diesels replaced steam locomotives on the Wallace run in 1954, and the following year the UP abandoned part of the original track which the W&I had constructed in 1889 between Tekoa,

Both the days of steam and the UP passenger service between Spokane and Wallace are numbered, but UP engine 3226 (a 4-6-2) puts on a gallant display as it heads train 67 out of Dishman, Washington, bound for Wallace. The date is April 22, 1953.

R. V. Nixon Photo

Train 67 a little further down the line near Mica, Washington.

Dr. Philip R. Hastings Photo

The beginning of the end of steam on the Wallace Branch of the UP. Here the former OWR&N 2-8-0 No. 732 runs only as a helper on Wallace bound evening freight 387. The main power is road engine No. 1250, a Baldwin-Westinghouse DRS 6-4-1500. The setting is Dishman, Washington, in June of 1951, and sun is fading — as is the future of steam.

Dr. Philip R. Hastings Photo

UP engine No. 1186, and Alco-GE RSC-2, leaves Spokane with train 67 on June 25, 1951. Apparently this steam replacement was only temporary, for — as other pictures in this chapter show — the passenger run to Wallace was operated by steam as late as 1953. Nevertheless, the diesel was soon to return, and the next time for good.

Ted Holloway Photo
Courtesy Maynard Rikerd

The retirement of steam on the UP's Wallace run was briefly interrupted in 1955 when 2-8-0 No. 6018 was called to wade through the flooding between Plummer and Wallace.

W. R. McGee Photo

NP's last regular passenger run to Wallace on April 18, 1941, at Huson, Montana. Note that No. 2212 is equipped with a pilot-mounted flanger (its long lever appears on the right side of the pilot — to the left in this photo).

R. V. Nixon Photo

The last passenger train beside the Clark Fork River at St. Regis, Montana, on April 18, 1941. Here the train is sitting on the track leading to Paradise, Montana, and the NP main line. In order to continue to Wallace the train must back up and then take the track leading off to the right.

Under Milwaukee wire the last passenger train passes an NP freight led by No. 4021 at Haugan, Montana.

Leaving Haugan No. 2212 will soon return to NP track as it continues the climb to the Idaho border.

This view shows the train crossing the highway and continuing around the curve leading to Borax and a water stop. Beyond Borax the line makes another 180-degree curve, this time to the right, and passes through the Borax tunnel. The track beyond the tunnel is the upper line visible in this photo. It continues up-grade to the right out of the picture.

The following day, April 19, 1941, the last Coeur d'Alene local returned to Missoula (shown here at the depot). The crew were engineer Fischer, fireman Haytin, and brakeman Harvey; and the cars used were numbers 164 and 1065.

Don Roberts Collection
Oregon Historical Society

Near the end of steam (October 25, 1953) NP No. 36 was still at work in Wallace. It had put in long service in Wallace and Missoula and was therefore one of three locomotives that were considered for donation to the city of Missoula a year and a half later. However it was not as glamorous as No. 1356 and therefore met the scrappers torch on July 29, 1957.

R. V. Nixon Photo

As steam engines were passing from the scene, Walter H. McLeod of Missoula worked to have an NP steamer donated to the city of Missoula. In April, 1955, Northern Pacific President Robert S. Macfarlane gave the go-ahead for the project. Engine No. 1356 was choosen, and after a complete restoration it was moved to a permanent display site in Missoula. This view shows 1356 being moved past the Missoula depot to the display. The date was October 17, 1955.

R. V. Nixon Photo

Retired after 1,115,000 miles of service, NP 1356 rests on display in Missoula where she can be seen to this day. The 1356 was a class S-4 ten-wheeler (4-6-0) built by Baldwin in 1902. Her initial assignment was to handle the North Coast Limited passenger train between Spokane and Missoula. In a short time the heavier Pacifics (4-6-2s) took over this task and 1356 was released to other duty. Her longest tour of duty was on the Coeur d'Alene Branch where she handled passenger and some freight trains. Near the end of passenger service on the branch she was again "bumped" by light Pacifics (such as No. 2212) which were in turn downgraded from main line service. One major change had been made in her appearance in January, 1917. As originally delivered she had been equipped with Vauclain compound cylinders, these were replaced with simple cylinders and a superheader was installed. Of all the steam engines that operated over the Coeur d'Alene Branch of the NP, just the 1356 and the 25 (a Y-1 class 2-8-0 which was donated to the city of Butte, Montana) were preserved.

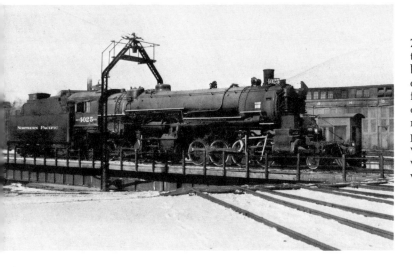

R. V. Nixon Photo

Z-3 No. 4025 on the Missoula turntable for the last time — February 10, 1955. Although No. 4025 probably handled more freights over Lookout Pass than any of the other Z-3s, it is interesting that she was absent from the run at the end of steam. Apparently she was overhauled and placed in storage at the Missoula roundhouse about 1953. Her clean appearance in this photo is evidence that she had seen little recent service. After leaving Missoula to be scrapped, 4025 survived until she met the torch on March 3, 1958. She was the last of the Z-3s used on the Coeur d'Alene Branch to go.

Washington, and Plummer, Idaho. This was done after the Milwaukee again granted the UP trackage rights over its line between Manito, Washington, and Plummer. Regular passenger service to Wallace by the UP lasted until the spring of 1957.

Most recently the UP acquired the Milwaukee track between Manito and Plummer in 1980 when the Milwaukee was forced into bankruptcy. Also this same year the UP took over the short section of BN track between Wallace and the Lucky Friday Mine (just above Mullan at the site of the old Gold Hunter Mine), thus bringing the Wallace Branch of the UP to its current operating length.

Like the UP, the NP also continued its reduction in mileage following the abandonments of 1934–1935 which were caused by the flood of 1933. The NP was able to drop its track between Wallace and Burke in 1938 (it was removed the next year) as the UP granted it trackage rights up its Canyon Creek track. Another great change occurred on April 19, 1941, when the UP dropped its regular passenger service from Missoula to Wallace. Notwithstanding this, the last

passenger run was actually a special train chartered for the GYRO organization between Wallace and Taft, Montana, on July 18, 1958.

In 1968 the remnant of the branch up Nine Mile Canyon was finally removed, and the NP also took steps to revitalize its line over Lookout Pass. Due to the deterioration of the wooden trestles and the high cost of their replacement (this was estimated at $500,000 for the "S" bridge alone), the NP had the spectacular "S" bridge, the "crown jewel" of the Coeur d'Alene Branch, permanently bypassed using the old switchback, and the bridge was sold for salvage. This landmark which was constructed in 1890 and repaired several times carried its last train across Willow Creek on October 16, 1963. In addition bridge 41.2, another trestle nearby, was also bypassed by a fill and removed. Although thousands of dollars were spent on this renovation, it only managed to postpone the fate of the line a few more years.

The NP was merged into the BN on March 3, 1970, along with the Great Northern; Chicago Burlington & Quincy; and the Spokane, Portland & Seattle. While the Coeur d'Alene

R. V. Nixon Photo

The last passenger train over the branch was this Gyro special of July 18, 1958. Here the train prepares to leave Wallace with an F7 at the point.

Branch continued operation, the BN viewed it as an expensive liability. Considering that the track over Lookout Pass was built as a "temporary" line (to be replaced by a tunnel), it was a wonder that it had operated as long as it had. Finally, after a number of delays, permission was granted for the BN to abandon the line from Wallace to St. Regis.

On a rainy, foggy autumn day (September 2, 1980) the last BN train, a 26-car freight with engineer Ken Powell and conductor Glenn Watters, rolled out of Wallace. Three of the cars carried one million dollars worth of ore apiece and the others were empty. No ceremony accompanied the passing of an era, just the gloom of the weather to fit the mood. It would seem that it deserved better.

R. V. Nixon Photo

The last passengers get a view of the beautiful "S" bridge as extra 6504, the Gyro special, works its way up the west side of Lookout Pass.

R.V. Nixon Photo

The last train crosses the "S" bridge before sunrise on October 16, 1963. Soon the line will bypass this landmark with the old switchback that originally allowed operation while the trestle was under construction. However, the new reason for the switchback is the high replacement cost of the aging structure.

R.V. Nixon Photo

Minutes after the passing of the last train the connecting track to the "S" bridge is removed. The once acclaimed engineering feat that is no more. "Progress" has passed it by like it has so many other things rich in history and full of beauty.

An Album of the Coeur d'Alenes

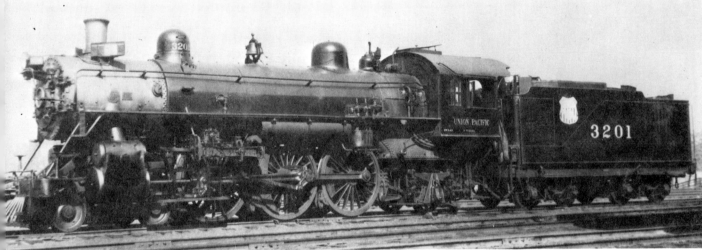

R. V. Nixon Photo

UP (OWR&N) No. 3201 in Spokane on October 1, 1931. This is an early view of one of the Pacifics (4-6-2s) that carried many passenger trains to the mining area. However, this was not the original appearance as this Baldwin (built in 1905) was originally equipped with compound cylinders.

R. V. Nixon Photo

UP (OWR&N) No. 1759 was a 4-6-0 that often worked the Wallace branch. The photograph was taken in April, 1932 in Spokane. The 1759 was built by Brooks in 1909 as a "Harriman Standard." This was a type of locomotive Edward Harriman (UP president) ordered standardized to cut costs.

Dr. Philip R. Hastings Photo

UP (former OWR&N) 2-8-0 No. 737 mounts the freight run-through line past Spokane's Union Station with freight No. 388 from Wallace on June 25, 1951.

W. R. McGee Photo

Wallace bound UP passenger train No. 67 passes through Dishman, Washington (just outside Spokane), with engine 3226 on the nineteenth of April, 1952.

R. V. Nixon Photo

UP engine No. 2894 (a 4-6-2) pauses at Mica, Washington, on January 9, 1953, with its three-car passenger train bound for Wallace.

R. V. Nixon Photo

A little further down the line at Rockford, Washington, train 67 nears the Idaho border. At this time (1953) both steam power and the Wallace passenger train had only a couple of years of service left.

Barnard-Stockbridge Collection
University of Idaho Library

This high drivered Atlantic (4-4-2) seems out of place in the mountainous country at Wallace as they were low on tractive effort (although very fast with light loads on a level grade). Surprisingly, the Wallace branch of the OWR&N did have many miles of level or near level grade. The worst grades were between Chatcolet and Tekoa, and these probably called for a helper when using an Atlantic. No. 3513 wasn't the only Atlantic used to Wallace, but it isn't clear how many were used. Engineer P. Sheeley took time from his oiling to pose for the photograph. His oil can is visible resting by the crosshead. The tender of 3513 carries the old UP emblem with the slogan "Overland Route." Behind the engine is evidence of the automobiles that were to ruin the passenger traffic — a Willy's Knight sign.

R. V. Nixon Photo

UP 4-6-2 No. 3224 takes on water at the tank just below Wallace. The track in the left foreground leads to the Wallace turntable and facilities. The date is April 17, 1946.

Barnard-Stockbridge Collection
University of Idaho Library

An unbelievably dirty OWR&N (UP) No. 723 is shown sitting on one of the turntable lead tracks at Wallace. (The lever to turn the Armstrong turntable shows at right.) The locomotive appears to have spent some time under an ore bin to have reached this condition. The locomotive was originally built by Baldwin in 1903 with Vauclain compound cylinders, but here is shown with replacement cylinders that appear to have come from a much older engine. The steam chest bears the initials OR&N.

Otto C. Perry Collection
Western History Department
Denver Public Library

UP 2-8-0 No. 742 photographed on September 28, 1931, just below Wallace at the UP yard. Part of the Hercules Mill appears in the background.

Don Roberts Collection
Oregon Historical Society

Heading a freight into Wallace September 5, 1945, is UP No. 735 (a 2-8-0).

Don Roberts Collection
Oregon Historical Society

Another "workhorse" 2-8-0 in Wallace was UP No. 737. This view of her was taken ca. 1950.

Dr. Philip R. Hastings Photo
UP (former OWR&N) 4-6-2 No. 3223 during a layover at the Wallace roundhouse after bringing in train 67 from Spokane, February 24, 1951.

Dr. Philip R. Hastings Photo
An unusual view of UP engine 3223 on the Wallace turntable showing a hostler packing a hot tender truck journal. After arriving from Spokane the tender was spotted on the turntable to give the workman a firm, dry place on which to work.

Dr. Philip R. Hastings Photo

Another unique view of No. 3223, this time taken from the Wallace roundhouse looking out at the engine receiving service.

Dr. Philip R. Hastings Photo

UP passenger train 67 from Spokane crosses the south fork of the Coeur d'Alene River and enters the Wallace yard on September 2, 1950. The train is handled by 4-6-2 No. 3219 carrying the UP's grey passenger colors.

Dr. Philip R. Hastings Photo

The end of run for train 67 is Wallace's UP depot on this second of September, 1950. Now the train can be readied for the return to Spokane.

R. V. Nixon Photo

Although spring had arrived (April 18, 1941) UP 2-8-0 No. 743 still sported a large pilot-mounted snowplow as she sat on a lead to the Wallace turntable.

Gayle Christen Photo

Not all UP passenger trains to Wallace featured beautifully kept motive power. As the 1950s progressed it was common to see engines like No. 3202, shown here pulling train 67 into Wallace.

Don Roberts Collection
Oregon Historical Society

At Kellogg (to the west of Wallace) UP 2-8-0 No. 732 was photographed on September 5, 1945.

Dr. Philip R. Hastings Photo

The date is September 11, 1950, and the sun is setting on UP's Spokane bound train 68 at Tekoa, Washington. In just a few short years the sun will also set on both steam power and passenger service to Wallace. Beyond the UP 4-6-2 No. 3219, which is handling the train, is the large steel viaduct of the CMStP&P (Milwaukee) main line.

Otto C. Perry Photo
Denver Public Library
Western History Department

NP No. 25 served many years in Wallace and is shown here about mid-career (September 28, 1931). The only major change in her later appearance would be the substitution of a different style tender. The location of this photo was the head of Nine Mile Canyon looking north. The NP depot was out of the picture to the right.

Don Roberts Collection
Oregon Historical Society

NP No. 36 (a class Y 2-8-0) was as familiar in Wallace as No. 25, for she served right up to the end of steam there (about 1955). Here she is shown on April 17, 1947, in the Wallace yard.

R. Levering Photo
W. R. McGee Collection

NP consolidation No. 24 was not used in Wallace as often as fellow class Y-1 No. 25, but here she is shown in the Wallace yard on April 15, 1939.

R. V. Nixon Photo

Class Z 2-6-6-6s No. 3001 and No. 3006 just out of the Livingston shop for service on the Coeur d'Alene Branch in the spring of 1925. It is of special note that this was one of Ron Nixon's first photos.

R. V. Nixon Photo

No. 3005 was another early NP class Z mallet used on the Wallace run. Here she is shown on December of 1931 at Missoula.

R. V. Nixon Photo

This ca. 1911 photograph taken in Missoula shows class Z No. 3014 with the older style tender. This engine was another of the slow moving 2-6-6-2s that boosted freights over Lookout Pass.

R. Levering Photo
W. R. McGee Collection

A later picture in Wallace (February 14, 1938) shows No. 3014 with the newer style tender.

R. Levering Photo
W. R. McGee Collection

Engine No. 3100 was the first of the class Z-1 mallets. She was sold to the Polson Logging Company in 1940, about two years after this photo was taken (May 20, 1938) in Wallace.

R. Levering Photo
W. R. McGee Collection

No. 3102 was another Z-1 engine that was used on the Coeur d'Alene Branch, photographed here in Wallace on March 22, 1938.

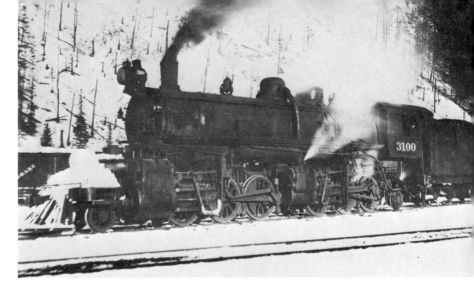

Saltese, Montana, was the probable location of this stark winter view of No. 3100 taken in 1913.

The Hunter Mill just above Mullan was the site of this shot of NP No. 3100 taken in September of 1937.

The Dorsey trestle just west of Lookout Pass was a great spot to photograph trains fighting the steep grade to the summit. Here the Missoula bound passenger is headed by 4-6-2 No. 2212.

Like all the rail lines much of the activity on the Coeur d'Alene Branch was far from glamorous. To keep the sleek passenger trains and massive freight engines operating the track required constant maintenance. Here a work train with a ditcher, gondola, and spreader heads upgrade across the "S" bridge over Willow Creek.

At the head of the work train 2-8-0 No. 64 stopped along the line as the ditcher sets to work.

The last view of the work train was probably taken by the water tank at Saltese. Here No. 64 is coupled to a "spreader."

This strange contraption was the NP's Rocky Mountain Division weed burner. Taken in 1899 (probably near Missoula), this is one of the earliest examples of this type of equipment. The locomotive (a 4-4-0 — possibly No. 886) and the flatcar operated as a set, but one must wonder how successful they could have been in this area that was plagued with forest fires.

Here the Wallace local is preparing to leave Missoula on October 13, 1939, with NP No. 1387 at the point. This same train was buried in a snow slide near Borax on February 29, 1935 (story told in Chapter Six).

The passenger train from Wallace sits on the right as the Northern Pacific Express No. 3 prepares to leave Missoula this day in 1903. The Express has a shiny new class Q 4-6-2 No. 297 in helper service followed by a class P-1 (a heavy 4-6-0 the Q class was soon to replace as the main power).

R. V. Nixon Photo

The Wallace local arriving in Missoula on November 1, 1939. Both the Ten Wheeler No. 1356 (heading the local) and the Consolidation No. 36 (in the background) were used extensively on the Coeur d'Alene Branch.

W. R. McGee Photo

Another view of 1387 about to head a Wallace bound No. 255 passenger out of Missoula February 14, 1941. The No. 255 was waiting for the No. 3 Alaskan which she had to follow out of town until the Coeur d'Alene Branch diverged from the main line at DeSmet, Montana.

R. V. Nixon Collection

DeSmet, Montana, six miles west of Missoula, was the point where the Coeur d'Alene Branch left the NP main line. Here, passing DeSmet with the Wallace local (No. 264) in April, 1932, is the famous Ten Wheeler No. 1356. This locomotive is now on display in Missoula.

Even the well-known rail photographer Otto Perry from faraway Colorado managed to photograph the Dorsey trestle on September 29, 1931. He captured this beautiful view of No. 1382 and her two-car passenger a few miles below Lookout Summit.

Class Y-1 2-8-0 No. 25 switching the Wallace NP yard prior to departing for road switching chores in the Wallace-Burke-Mullan district on September 2, 1950. In the background are the idle buildings of the Hercules Mill.

Dr. Philip R. Hastings Photo

Another view of No. 25 switching the Wallace yard on
September 2, 1950.

R. V. Nixon Photo

No. 4021 extra west crossing U.S. Highway 10 near Borax, Montana. Note the unusual appearance of the boiler
front with only one compound air pump rather than the normal two, September 28, 1945.

Dr. Philip R. Hastings Photo

The Wallace NP roundhouse framed by the caboose of the local freight with the Hercules Mill in the background, September 2, 1950.

R. V. Nixon Photo

Z-3 No. 4020 following maintenance at Missoula is readied for her return to Wallace this July 6, 1950. NP dispatchers Phil Coulter and George Lamb (left to right) pose in the foreground.

Dr. Philip R. Hastings Photo

No. 4021 blasts away from Saltese, Montana headed for Lookout Pass 14 miles of four percent grade in the distance, and then 20 more miles down the other side to Wallace, Idaho, September 2, 1950.

Dr. Philip R. Hastings Photo

The westbound freight with NP engine No. 4021 on the grade approaching the stop at Borax, Montana. Z-3 engines Nos. 4020, 4021, 4024, and 4025 called the Coeur d'Alene Branch home in the later years of steam, and one made a daily round trip of 114 miles to St. Regis, Montana and return.

Dr. Philip R. Hastings Photo

A water stop at the Borax, Montana tank provides a brief rest for No. 4021 on its westward climb up the four percent grade to Lookout, September 2, 1950.

R.V. Nixon Photo

Z-3 No. 4025 preparing to leave St. Regis, Montana on April 14, 1943, with the westbound freight to Wallace, Idaho. The Clark Fork River appears behind the engine.

R.V. Nixon Photo

Having climbed from the river level, NP Extra West joins the Milwaukee line (the Milwaukee bridge over the Clark Fork shows in background) as the train leaves St. Regis April 14, 1943.

R.V. Nixon Photo

Here NP's westbound Wallace local waits at Henderson, Montana for this meet with Milwaukee No. 16 on June 13, 1951.

Having taken on water in 4021, the fireman flings up the spout on the Borax tank.

R.V. Nixon Photo

Haugan, Montana was the end of the NP's joint track-age rights with the Milwaukee, and here No. 4025 again rejoins the NP track to Wallace on April 14, 1943.

W.R. McGee Photo

Two miles east of Saltese, Montana the Milwaukee track still appears across the St. Regis River from the NP line. Soon the Milwaukee track climbs away from the river, cuts through the mountains at the St. Paul tunnel, and emerges in the St. Joe River country. This view shows NP No. 4025 approaching Saltese on April 18, 1952.

W.R. McGee Photo

Having taken on fuel at the Saltese coaling tower in the background, 4025 resumes her journey to Lookout and Wallace on April 18, 1952.

Dr. Philip R. Hastings Photo

The awesome power required to battle up the four percent grade is graphically illustrated in this picture taken west of Saltese. The Z-3's massive front end with dual compound air pumps, huge cylinders, and low slung headlight; the billowing clouds of black smoke; and the short train limited to 600 tons, almost thunder out of this photograph taken on July 3, 1951.

R. V. Nixon Photo

Another westbound freight headed by No. 4025 crosses U.S. Highway 10 on July 31, 1951, just below Borax.

R.V. Nixon Photo
Lookout Summit comes into view on July 31, 1951, as 4025 struggles the last yards to the top.

R.V. Nixon Photo
Decending the four percent west of Lookout No. 4025 crosses one of the smaller trestles April 14, 1943. Note the intermediate bents that had been added to strengthen the old structure. Also notice the tall poles along U.S. 10 which aided the highway snowplows in the wintertime. Today this highway is a four-lane engineering marvel that for years was considered impossible to build.

Don Roberts Collection
Oregon Historical Society

May 30, 1951, NP Z-3 No. 4025 sits steaming in the Wallace yard under the sanding tower.

R. V. Nixon Photo

An unidentified eastbound Z-3 crosses the "S" bridge with an unusually long (for Lookout Pass) train in tow.

R. V. Nixon Photo

No 4025 and her eastbound train are silhouetted as they cross the Dorsey trestle near the summit on April 7, 1944. Again notice the additional bents added to strengthen the upper portion of the trestle.

This eastbound one-car freight pauses at Lookout Summit June 13, 1951.

NP No. 4025 Extra East crossing U.S. 10 just below Borax, Montana on April 15, 1943.

No. 4025 follows the St. Regis River east near the site of the old town of Taft, Montana. On this April day (fifteenth) in 1943 much of the snow has yet to melt and spring track work is getting underway.

W. R. McGee Photo

NP engine No. 1387 at speed nearing DeSmet on August 8, 1939, heading train 256 from Wallace for a Missoula connection with the North Coast Limited. One would hope that the excitement of these days — when the Coeur d'Alene Branch was at its height — will be a lasting memory.

Appendix A

Chronology

Date	Spokane Falls & Idaho RR	Coeur d'Alene Ry. & Navigation Co.	Northern Pacific RR	(Union Pacific) Washington & Idaho RR	Miscellaneous
April 22, 1886		articles of incorporation			
June, 1886		construction begun			
July, 1886	NP agrees to do work				
July 6, 1886		incorporation filed in Montana			
July 12, 1886				incorporated in Washington	
Mid-Aug., 1886	formal contract with NP				
Oct. 4, 1886	tracklaying begun				
Oct. 22, 1886				surveyed to Old Mission	
Oct. 24, 1886	incorporated in Washington as SF&I — trains run to Coeur d'Alene waterfront				
Nov., 1, 1886		tracklaying begun 40 lb. steel			
Nov. 9, 1886	turned over to operators				
Dec. 25, 1886		finished to Wardner Junction — operation stopped after one week			
Mar. 20, 1887		operation reopened to Wardner Junction			
July 14, 1887					Canyon Creek RR incorporated
Sept. 5, 1887		Canyon Creek RR purchased			
Sept. 10, 1887		track reaches Wallace — injunction ties up 1½ miles			
Sept. 30, 1887		celebration at Wallace			
Oct. 1, 1887	SF&I leased to NP				
Oct. 29, 1887		injunction on track dissolved			
Nov. 2, 1887		first regular train to Wallace			
Dec. 22, 1887		Canyon Creek Railroad in operation — celebration at Burke			
Mid-May, 1888				senate bill granted right-of-way across Coeur d'Alene Indian Reservation became law	
May 18, 1888				franchise transferred to OR&N	
June 1, 1888				sod broken Farmington-Spokane Falls-Coeur d' Alene mines	
June 30, 1888			NP hires men to stall W&I		
August 4, 1888			surveying Nine Mile Canyon		
Sept. 14, 1888		leased to the NP			

Date	Spokane Falls & Idaho RR	Coeur d'Alene Ry. & Navigation Co.	Northern Pacific RR	(Union Pacific) Washington & Idaho RR	Miscellaneous
Oct. 1, 1888		NP assumes control			
Feb. 8, 1889				Farmington-Rockford completed, permission granted to cross reservation	
March 24, 1889		narrow gauge reaches Mullan			
April, 1889			survey completed up Fourth of July Canyon		
June 18, 1889		narrow gauge reaches Hunter Mill			
Oct. 15, 1889				Rockford-Spokane Falls complete	
Nov. 19, 1889				track to Wardner Junction	
Dec. 9, 1889				W&I reaches Wallace	
Dec. 23, 1889				first passenger train Wallace to Spokane Falls	
Jan. 17, 1890			Coeur d'Alene Branch started, track 6 miles west Frenchtown		
March 30, 1890				Wallace-Mullan finished	
April 15, 1890					Wallace & Sunset incorporated, Wardner Mining RR incorporated
June 4, 1890			agreement between NP and UP about W&I building up Canyon Creek Canyon		
Nov. 18, 1890				construction to Burke began track through Burke to Poorman Concentrator	
Dec. 22, 1890			last spike driven Coeur d'Alene Branch		
Dec. 23, 1890			first train Missoula-Mullan, celebration in Wallace		
July 23, 1891		last narrow gauge train Wallace to Mullan			
August 14, 1891			first freight Missoula-Wallace		
by end of 1891			5 miles graded up Nine Mile — Burke Branch now standard gauge		
June 11, 1892					work begun Morning Mine RR
August 15, 1893			1893 panic puts the NP into receivership		
Oct. 10, 1893		Henry Stanton & John Huntoon appointed receivers CR&N			
Spring, 1894			track Wallace-Missoula not in operation until late July	track Wallace-Mullan abandoned due to flooding	heavy flooding
Sept. 20, 1895				action to foreclose on W&I begun	
— 1896 —			NPRR reorganized as the NP *Railway*		
Sept. 1, 1896		receivers leased CR&N to the Northern Pacific Railway			
Jan. 26, 1897		CR&N purchased by NP			
March 2, 1898		start of track removal — Old Mission to Wardner Junction			
Dec. 9, 1898					Idaho Northern RR incorporated
April 29, 1899					Bunker Hill smelter dynamited
May 26, 1899					Idaho Northern surveys completed
— 1901 —				Sierra Nevada Branch built	
— 1902 —		track removed Wardner Junction to Wallace			

Date	Spokane Falls & Idaho RR	Coeur d'Alene Ry. & Navigation Co.	Northern Pacific RR	(Union Pacific) Washington & Idaho RR	Miscellaneous
May 20, 1902			new (present) NP depot in Wallace opened		
Oct. 20, 1902					Coeur d'Alene & Spokane Ry. (electric) incorporated
Dec. 28, 1903					C&S line opened
July 26, 1906					Lake Creek & Coeur d' Alene Ry. incorporated (Amwaco Branch)
Dec. 30, 1908					first Idaho Northern train to Murray — celebration
— 1909 —					Lake Creek & Coeur d' Alene construction begun — Idaho Northern completed Enaville to Paragon
Feb. 6, 1909			new line St. Regis to Paradise opened		
June 12, 1910					Lake Creek & Coeur d'Alene opened
Aug. 20, 1910					great 1910 forest fire
Dec. 23, 1910				all UP subsidiary lines in North Idaho merged with OR&N and reorganized as Oregon-Washington RR & Navigation Co.	
March 1, 1911				Idaho Northern RR taken over by OWR&N — operated as IN branch	
Oct. 1, 1916				work started on Beaver Creek Branch off Idaho Northern	
Feb., 1917				Beaver Creek Branch completed	
— 1918 —				IN track Prichard-Paragon abandoned due to flood 1917	
July 13, 1923					fire at Burke destroys most of town
Sept. 20, 1923			last local passenger train Wallace-Larson (above Mullan)		
July 21, 1926			last local passenger train (Sat. nights) to Burke		
— 1932 —				Amwaco and Beaver branches abandoned	
Dec., 1933			due to flood NP starts using Milwaukee track St. Regis to Haugan	Idaho Northern washed out — Pine Creek Spur damaged	terrific flooding
— 1934 —			Bunn-Sunset (Nine Mile Canyon) abandoned 2.27 miles	Pine Creek Spur abandoned	
→ 1935 —			St. Regis-Haugan abandoned 18.37 miles	Idaho Northern Branch abandoned 20.64 miles	
— 1936 —				Union Pacific leases OWR&N	
— 1938 —			UP grants NP trackage rights between Wallace and Burke		
— 1939 —			Wallace-Burke abandoned 6.23 miles		
— 1941 —				Sierra Nevada Branch cut to 3.24 miles	
April 19, 1941			last regular passenger train Wallace-Missoula		
— 1953 —				Sierra Nevada Branch cut to 2 miles	
— 1955 —				UP obtains right over Milwaukee track Manite-Plummer-Tekoa-Plummer abandoned	
July 18, 1958			GYRO special last passenger train Coeur d'Alene Branch		
Oct. 16, 1963			last train uses "S" bridge		
March 3, 1970			NP taken over in BN merger		

Date	Spokane Falls & Idaho RR	Coeur d'Alene Ry. & Navigation Co.	Northern Pacific RR	(Union Pacific) Washington & Idaho RR	Miscellaneous
Fall, 1980				UP purchases Milwaukee's line Manite, Washington-Plummer, Idaho	
Sept. 2, 1980			last BN train leaves Wallace on Coeur d'Alene Branch	UP takes over BN track Wallace to Lucky Friday mine	
Fall, 1981			track torn up Haugan, Montana to Mullan, Idaho		

Appendix B

Selected Locomotive Rosters

*Bunker Hill & Sullivan Smelter — standard gauge

No.	Builder	Year	C/N	Type	Cyls. H.P.	Dri.	From	To	Notes
					Steam Locomotives				
1	Porter	5/1916	5662	0-4-0T	11x16	?	new	scr?	
2	?	?	?	?	?	?	?	?	
3	Alco (Cooke)	5/1919	60560	0-6-0T	17x24	?	new	scr?	A
4	Alco (Cooke)	9/1923	65281	0-6-0T	17x24	?	new	scr?	
5	Lima	10/1920	6001	0-6-0	?	?	UP #4464 7/7/54	scr?	
6	Baldwin	3/1918	48079	0-6-0	?	?	UP #4434 7/7/54	scr?	
					Internal Combustion Locomotives				
630	Plymouth	9/1950	5538	B	33½hp		new?		B
631	?	?	?	?	?		?	?	
632	G.E.	12/1941	15052	B-B	300hp		new		C
633	G.E.	5/1956	32535	B-B	300hp		new		C
634	G.E.	5/1956	32534	B-B	300hp		new		C
639	Plymouth	1942	?	B	?		?		D
640	Whitcomb	1941	?	B	?		A.D. Schader Co.		E
?	Whitcomb	8/1943	60282	B-B	500hp		USA #7850 9/46	Pan-Am Eng/57	
					Electrics				
1	Baldwin	10/1916	44296	B	20hp		new		
2	Baldwin	10/1916	44297	B	20hp		new		
M-3	Baldwin	10/1916	44185	B	100hp		new		

Notes: A — 59 or 60 ton, B — *24″ gauge*, 5 ton, C — 45 ton, D — Fate Roote Heath Co. type 3, Model ML-6, 20 ton, changed to diesel, used as slagmotor. E — Model ADR, 20 ton, changed to diesel, used as slagmotor.

*Coeur d'Alene Railway & Navigation Company — 3′ gauge

Steam Locomotives

No.	Builder	Year	C/N	Type	Cyls.	Dri.	From	To	Notes
1	Grant	1/1881	1484	2-6-0	13x18	42″	T&St.L #18 9/86	M&O 2/#	A
2	Grant	6/1881	1504	2-6-0	13x18	42″	T&St.L #29 9/86	M&O 2/#2	B
3	Baldwin	?	?	2-6-0	?	?	? 1887	H&S	C
4	Baldwin	2/1889	9836	2-6-0	16x24	48″	new	EBT #9 12/92	D

Notes: A — ex. Texas & St. Louis "John Parham," to Mason & Oceana (in 1898?). B — T&St.L "Wm. Cameron," to M&O (in 1898?). C — sold 2/1893 to James Richardson for $2076 to Huston & Shreveport Ry. D — East Broad Top RR & Coal Co. in turn sold engine to Males Co. (used equipment dealer) 12/1915.

Other Equipment

In a report to the stock exchange on May 14, 1889, the CR&N listed two passenger cars (coaches), 21 boxcars, 36 flatcars, three steamboats, and two barges — these in addition to the four locomotives.

*Hecla Mining Co. — 24″ gauge?

Steam Locomotives

No.	Builder	Year	C/N	Type	Cyls.	Dri.	From	To	Notes
16	?	?	?	0-4-0T	?	?	Anaconda Copper?	scr?	A
17	Porter	12/1896	1715	0-4-0T	6x10	0	Standard Mining	scr?	B

Notes: A — a photo taken 2/23/48 stated engine out of service. B — built as compressed air engine, converted to steam at Hecla shop, original gauge 18″ also apparently changed to 24″.

Other Locomotives

In addition to these two narrow gauge engines, the Hecla had a standard gauge self-propelled steam crane. Also there are several internal combustion locomotives currently used on the narrow gauge track.

*Idaho Northern Railroad — standard gauge

Steam Locomotives

No.	Builder	Year	C/N	Type	Cyls.	Dri.	From	To	Notes
1	Rhode Isl.	/1890	2451	4-4-0	18x26	64″	OR&N #87 8/7/09	OWR&N 3/1/11	A
2	NY (Rome)	10/1889	430	2-8-0	20x24	51″	OR&N #161	OWR&N 3/1/11	B

Notes: A — became UP #1121, retired 10/1925. B — 109 ton, became UP 701, scrap 4/1929.

*Morning Mine Railroad (became Larson & Greenough) — 3′ gauge

Steam Locomotives

No.	Builder	Year	C/N	Type	Cyls.	Dri.	From	To	Notes
1	Lima	8/11/92	405	2-tr. Shay	9x8	27″	new	Fernwood Lbr. Co.	A
2	Lima	10/21/96	522	2-tr. Shay	11x12	32″	new	PSM&ECo.	B
2/1	Lima	11/ 6/97	538	2-tr. Shay	12x12	32″	new	PSM&ECo.	C

Notes: A — Shay records list C/N 405 as standard gauge, but this must be in error as the Morning Mine track was always 3′ gauge — sold to FLCo. #4, Fernwood, Miss.; to Red Creek L. Co., Lumberton, Miss.; to Holman & Batson L. Co., Lyman, Miss. B — sold to Puget Sound Mills & Timber Co., Port Angeles, Wash.; to Hofius Steel & Equip. Co., Seattle, Wash. 2/10/31; scr. 1931. C — purchased by Larson & Greenough — sold to PSM&E; to Hofius; to J. A. Fortier Inc. (dealer) Seattle, Wash. 2/28; conv. to std. Washington Lumber & Spar Co., Newcastle, Wash.; scr. 1931.

*National Mining Co. — 42″ gauge

Electric Locomotive

No.	Builder	Year	C/N	Type	H.P.	From	To	Notes
1	Baldwin-West	7/03	22573	B	100hp	new	?	

*Standard Mining Co. — 18″ gauge

Compressed Air Locomotive

No.	Builder	Year	C/N	Type	Cyls.	Dri.	From	To	Notes
?	Porter	12/1896	1715	0-4-0	6x10	?	new	Hecla Mining #17	

Bibliography

Books and Phamphlets

Abdill, George B., *Pacific Slope Railroads*, Seattle, Washington: Superior Publishing Company, 1959.

———, *Rails West*, Seattle, Washington: Superior Publishing Company, 1960.

———, *This Was Railroading*, Seattle, Washington: Superior Publishing Company, 1958.

Adams, Kramer, *Logging Railroads of the West*, Seattle, Washington: Superior Publishing Company, 1961.

Athearn, Robert G., *Union Pacific Country*, Chicago: Rand McNally and Company, 1971.

Bankson, Russell A. and Harrison, Lester S., *Beneath These Mountains*, New York: Vantage Press, 1966.

Beal, Merrill D., *Intermountain Railroads — Standard and Narrow Gauge*, Caldwell, Idaho: The Caxton Printers, Ltd., 1962.

Bryan, Enoch Albert, *Orient Meets Occident*, Pullman, Washington: The Student's Book Corporation, 1936.

Ehernberger, James L. and Gschwind, Francis G., *Smoke Along the Columbia*, Callaway, Nebraska: E. and G. Publications, 1968.

Fahey, John, *The Ballyhoo Bonanza — Charles Sweeny and the Idaho Mines*, Seattle, Washington: University of Washington Press, 1971.

———, *The Days of the Hercules*, Moscow, Idaho: University of Idaho Press, 1978.

———, *Inland Empire — D. C. Corbin and Spokane*, Seattle, Washington: University of Washington Press, 1965.

Fleming, Howard, *Narrow Gauge Railways in America*, ed. by Grahame Hardy and Paul Darrell, Oakland, California: G. H. Hardy, 1949.

Greenough, W. Earl, *The Coeur d'Alene Mining Region 1849–1949*, Mullan, Idaho: W. Earl Greenough, 1947.

Hedges, James Blaine, *Henry Villard and the Railways of the Northwest*, New Haven, Connecticut: Yale University Press, 1930.

Henderson, John M., Shiach, William S., and Averill, Harry B., *An Illustrated History of North Idaho*, Chicago: Western Historical Publishing Company, 1903.

Hult, Ruby El, *Steamboats in the Timber*, Caldwell, Idaho: The Caxton Printers, Ltd., 1952.

Inland Empire Railway Review — Northern Pacific and Spokane 1881–1981, Spokane, Washington: The Inland Empire Railway Historical Society, 1981.

Kratville, William W. and Ranks, Harold E., *Motive Power of the Union Pacific*, Omaha, Nebraska: Barnhart Press, 1958.

Kyper, Frank, *A Ramble into the Past on the East Broad Top Railroad*, Rockhill Furnace, Pennsylvania: The East Broad Top Railroad and Coal Company, 1971.

Livingston-Little, Dallas E., *An Economic History of North Idaho, 1800–1900*, Los Angeles: Lorrin L. Morrison and Carroll Spear Morrison, 1965.

Magnuson, Richard G., *Coeur d'Alene Dairy*, Portland, Oregon: Metropolitan Press, 1968.

Mineral County Historical Book 1976, Superior, Montana: Mineral County Historical Society, 1976.

Norman, Sidney, *Northwest Mines Handbook*, Spokane, Washington: Sidney Norman, 1918.

Rainbow Seekers — A KXLY Publication, ed. Joseph C. Brown, Spokane, Washington: Wescoast Publishing Company, 1974.

Richard, T. A., *The Bunker Hill Enterprise*, San Francisco: Mining and Scientific Press, 1921.

Smith, Robert Wayne, *The Coeur d'Alene Mining War of 1892*, Corvallis, Oregon: Oregon State University Press, 1961.

Spencer, Betty Goodwin, *The Big Blowup*, Caldwell, Idaho: The Caxton Printers, Ltd., 1956.

Stell, William T., *Silver Strike*, Boston: Little, Brown, and Company, 1932.

Strong, Clarence C. and Webb, Clyde S., *White Pine: King of Many Waters*, Missoula, Montana: Mountain Press Publishing Company, 1970.

Wheeler, Olin D., *6,000 Miles Through Wonderland: Being a Description of the Marvelous Region Traversed by the Northern Pacific Railroad*, Chicago: Rand McNally and Company, 1893.

Welle, Muriel Sibell, *Montana Pay Dirt*, Denver: Sage Books, 1963.

Wood, Charles R., *The Northern Pacific: Main Street of the Northwest*, Seattle, Washington: Superior Publishing Company, 1968.

Articles

Day, Henry L., "Mining Highlights of the Coeur d'Alene District," *Idaho Yesterdays,* 7, No. 4 (Winter, 1963–64), 2–9.

Garber, C. Y., "Fire on Pine Creek," *Idaho Yesterdays,* 11, No. 2 (Summer, 1967), 27–30.

Hubbard, Freeman, "Interesting Railfans No. 76 — Ronald V. Nixon," *Railroad Magazine,* April, 1969, 24–28.

Kizer, Benjamin H., "May Arkwright Hutton," *Pacific Northwest Quarterly,* 57, No. 2 (April, 1966), 49–56.

Government Publications

Jones, Edward L., Jr., "A Reconnaissance of the Pine Creek District, Idaho," USGS *Bulletin 710A,* Washington: GPO, 1919.

Ransome, Frederick Leslie, and Frank Cathcart Calkins, "Geology and Ore Deposits of the Coeur d'Alene District, Idaho," USGS *Professional Paper 62,* Washington: GPO, 1908.

Umpleby, Joseph B., and E. L. Jones, Jr., "Geology and Ore Deposits of Shoshone County, Idaho," USGS *Bulletin 732,* Washington: GPO, 1923.

Newspapers

Coeur d'Alene Miner (Wallace, Idaho)

Coeur d'Alene Press

Daily Missoulian (Missoula, Montana)

Helena Independent

Idaho Press (Wallace, Idaho) also *Daily Idaho Press*

Kellogg Evening News

North Idaho Press (Wallace, Idaho)

Press-Times (Wallace, Idaho)

Spokane Daily Chronicle

Spokesman-Review (Spokane, Washington)

Wallace Free Press

Wallace Miner

Wallace Press

Other Periodicals

Inland Empire Rail Quarterly, Spokane, Washington (Inland Empire Railway Historical Society)

Poor's Manual of Railroads, New York

Railway Age Gazette, Chicago

Yardbull Newsletter, Spokane, Washington (monthly publication of the Inland Empire Railway Historical Society)

Unpublished

The Minnesota Historical Society supplied copies of various unpublished materials from the Northern Pacific Railway records. These included minutes of the meetings of the Board of Directors for the Coeur d'Alene Railway and Navigation Company, maps of that line, and its annual reports. Also provided were selected annual reports of the Northern Pacific and correspondence of NP officials concerning the Coeur d'Alene Branch.

Index

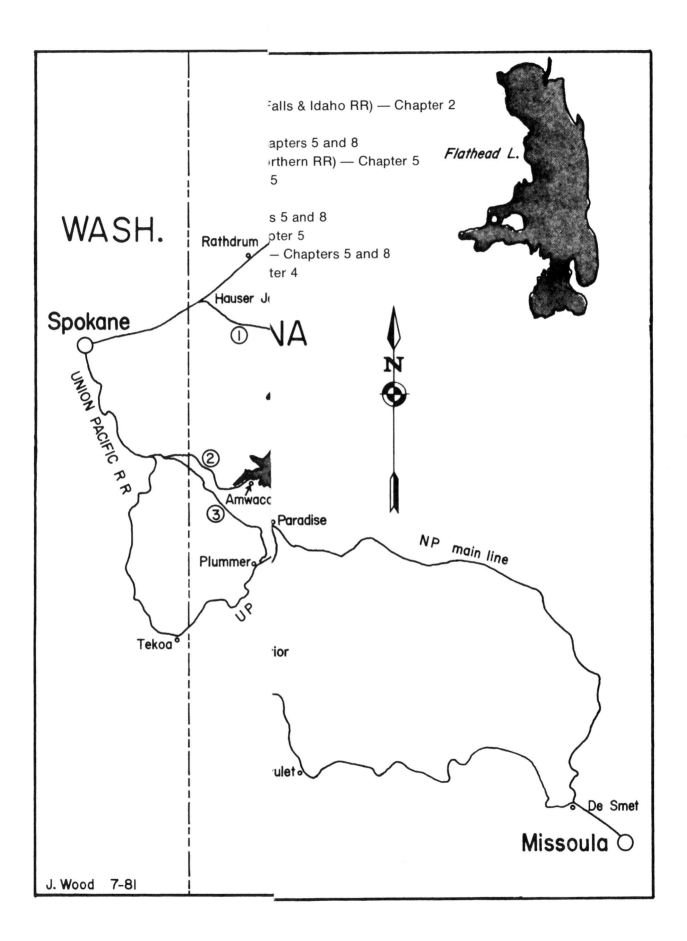

WASH.

Rathdrum

Hauser J<

Spokane

①

UNION PACIFIC R R

②

Amwaco

③

Paradise

Plummer

U P

Tekoa

·ior

·ulet

Flathead L.

N

Falls & Idaho RR) — Chapter 2

apters 5 and 8
orthern RR) — Chapter 5
5

s 5 and 8
oter 5
— Chapters 5 and 8
ter 4

·NA

NP main line

De Smet

Missoula